SW

MW00584357

AT

BIRTH

SWITCHED
AT
BIRTH

Jessica
Pitchford

Jonathan Ball Publishers

Johannesburg & Cape Town

Were it not for *60 Minutes Australia* this book would not have been written: thanks to Howard, Micky, Gareth and the late Richard Carleton for reminding us that some stories are worth travelling the globe to find. And to *Carte Blanche* which has, over the years, featured several baby swap stories, two of which provided material for this book.

Originally published in South Africa in 2016 by
JONATHAN BALL PUBLISHERS (PTY) LTD
A division of Media24 Limited
P O Box 33977
Jeppestown
2043

ISBN 978-1-86842-672-0
Ebook 978-1-86842-673-7

Twitter: http://www.twitter.com/JonathanBallPub
Facebook: http://www.facebook.com/JonathanBallPublishers
Blog: http://jonathanball.bookslive.co.za/

Cover design by publicide
Design and typesetting by Lauren Rycroft
Typeset in 12.5 pt Bembo

Printed by *paarlmedia*, a division of Novus Holdings

Contents

Clinton-Parker

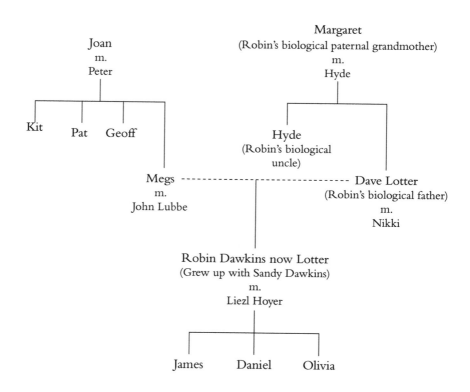

Joan
m.
Peter

Margaret
(Robin's biological paternal grandmother)
m.
Hyde

Kit   Pat   Geoff

Hyde
(Robin's biological
uncle)

Megs
m.
John Lubbe

Dave Lotter
(Robin's biological father)
m.
Nikki

Robin Dawkins now Lotter
(Grew up with Sandy Dawkins)
m.
Liezl Hoyer

James   Daniel   Olivia

Dawkins

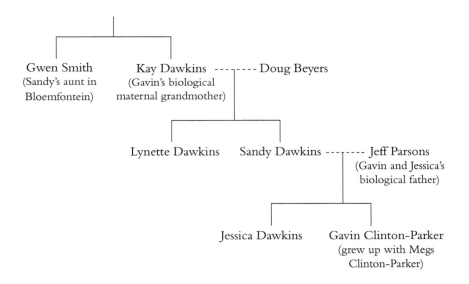

Gwen Smith
(Sandy's aunt in
Bloemfontein)

Kay Dawkins -------- Doug Beyers
(Gavin's biological
maternal grandmother)

Lynette Dawkins   Sandy Dawkins ------- Jeff Parsons
(Gavin and Jessica's
biological father)

Jessica Dawkins   Gavin Clinton-Parker
(grew up with Megs
Clinton-Parker)

Foreword

My association with Megs and Sandy, Gavin and Robin goes back 20 years. In the early 1990s, I occasionally did freelance fixing for *60 Minutes Australia*, a current affairs programme with budgets grand enough to be able to travel far and wide to tell personal stories that transcend borders. When producer Howard Sacre first asked me to track down two South African mothers whose children had been switched at birth in a hospital near Johannesburg, I was initially surprised by the interest in what to me seemed a slightly inconsequential South African story.

As a news journalist I was obsessed with the bigger picture: the transition to democracy, Mandela's charm offensive and South Africa's return to the world stage. But this assignment turned out to be the start of a relationship with an unusual family unit in which I was the go-between: setting up shoots, organising venues, smoothing ruffled feathers. The boys' seventh birthday party was filmed at my house.

Years passed in which I had little contact with the mothers and their sons, instead following their lives in magazine and newspaper articles. When I met up with them again, with a view to writing this book, the boys were young men with nothing in common except two mothers still deeply affected by the actions of a careless nurse in the summer of 1989.

This is their story; a story that has had lasting consequences for the lives of two families.

Jessica Pitchford
Johannesburg, 2016

Prologue

In February 1989, two women who didn't know each other, and in all probability would never have met, gave birth at the Nigel Hospital, in the then Transvaal Province. Megs Clinton-Parker's son arrived first – at 3.45 pm.

Her mother, Joan, jotted down the details of her grandson's arrival on a pad next to the phone:

17/2/89 GAVIN JOHN; 3.3kg; 47cm; head 35cm.

Megs' pregnancy had been a shock: having a baby out of wedlock simply wasn't in the Clinton-Parker family lexicon. Joan (who had been nicknamed 'Primmy' at university) was a Pietermaritzburg schoolteacher and Megs' father Peter was an engineer with the City Council. She had three siblings, sisters Kit and Pat and brother Geoff and they lived in a big old Victorian house in Scottsville.

Megs managed a photographic studio. She was sociable and confident, but her predicament made things really difficult, as she recalls:

'Falling pregnant at age 27 was embarrassing. I should have known better. I felt as if I had let the side down, especially my mum and dad. It was my mum's job as a senior English teacher of long standing to counsel her pupils against foolish mistakes in life and yet here I was almost defying her by making it look as though she couldn't even counsel her own daughter.'

Six months later Megs had left her comfort zone and got a temporary job at a photographic studio in Pretoria, staying at a residential hotel. Advanced pregnancy didn't go well with the summer heat in the capital – and it aggravated her lymphedema, a condition inherited from her mother that caused water retention and swelling.

'I stuck it out for two months until it was almost time to have the baby,' she recalls. 'It was easier just to get away. My older sister Kit lived in Nigel on the East Rand, she was teaching at a school there. I went to stay with her when it was time …'

A letter from the Nigel Hospital, dated 19 January 1989, advises Megs to bring 'one cake toilet soap and two safety pins' with her, as well as her personal items. But Megs doesn't remember much about the hospital at all: 'I probably blanked that out years ago,' she admits.

★

The maternity ward's other occupant on 17 February 1989 was Sandy Dawkins, who went into labour shortly before seven in the morning.

Twenty-six-year-old Sandy lived in Nigel with her boyfriend Jeff. He was English-speaking, she was Afrikaans. She'd left school before finishing and worked as a bank clerk in the Johannesburg city centre. She was looking forward to having her first child. Jeff, a handyman, already had two children from a previous marriage.

Apart from an insatiable craving for pineapple at the start and skyrocketing blood pressure near the end, Sandy's pregnancy had been uneventful.

'Jeff and I set off for the hospital in pouring rain,' she remembers. 'The weather suited the miserable attitude of the nurses, who seemed to find my presence there an inconvenience. They grumbled and mumbled and didn't make me feel at ease, even though I told them I was a first-time mum. Anyway, they shaved me, gave me painkillers and an enema and later when I couldn't take it any more, a pethidine injection. When I wanted to go to the loo at about three in the afternoon they told me to hold on as delivery was very close. But the delivery room was occupied, so they took me to a theatre used for applying plaster of Paris.'

★

In the delivery room, Megs Clinton-Parker held her newborn baby while doctors stitched her.

'I was given pethidine during labour,' she says, 'but wasn't offered a local anaesthetic and every time a stitch was inserted, I'd squeeze him to better manage the pain ... I was worried I would squeeze the life out of him, so I handed him over to a nurse to be washed. The pethidine made me throw up for the next hour.'

Later that evening, Megs and her sister visited the nursery. Kit had been present for most of the labour but had slipped out to take care of her own four-month-old son. She'd arrived back at the hospital just in time to see her nephew being born. Now she walked over to the blond child she thought was him. But he was tagged 'Dawkins'.

★

Sandy's baby was born after an episiotomy and 'three mighty pushes'. His most prominent feature, observed his mum, watching him being held upside-down, was his black hair.

Jeff didn't get a good look at all. His attention was on Sandy. The doctor had told him to make himself useful and hold a mask over Sandy's nose. Except the cylinder of laughing gas was empty and she kept swatting him away, saying he was suffocating her. So he didn't remember anything about the baby at all.

Sandy got stitched while her newborn boy went to be washed. She recalls a nurse later placing him in her arms and being surprised by his wisps of blond hair. And to hear he'd weighed only 3.04 kilograms.

'I found that odd because during my pregnancy I was huge. But I didn't argue, although I told the nurse I thought he'd had black hair. She said their hair always looked black at birth because of the blood. I held him for a while before they took him away so I could have something to eat: soup, bread, curry and rice, some grapes and a cup of coffee. I tucked in heartily then was almost immediately violently ill.'

She visited the nursery later that night. There were three babies, all in incubators. She made her way to the child she knew was hers.

'I walked over to his incubator, but was told by the nurse that wasn't him; he was in the corner incubator. I must have looked doubtful because she said if I didn't believe her I should check the other baby's tag. It said "Dawkins".'

Somehow on that summer evening in Nigel, the dark-haired Baby Dawkins had become Baby Clinton-Parker – and a few days later, the two little boys, named Gavin and Robin, went home with the wrong mothers.

The First Meeting

Megs had known Dave Lotter since high school. They'd met via Citizen Band radio, which was to communication in the seventies and eighties what mobile phones are to the twenty-first century.

Dave came from a dysfunctional family. He and his brother Hyde were afraid of their father. He was abusive towards them and their mother Margaret, who eventually divorced him. She and Megs later struck up a friendship – they shared a birthday and the same first name.

Dave loved the stability and warmth of the Clinton-Parker household. Megs, Kit, Pat and Geoff had loads of friends, and pretty girls flooded their double-storey house. Dave in turn kept them entertained, dressing up in drag and high heels on occasion, prancing around Pietermaritzburg.

'We always did a lot of laughing when Dave was around,' the youngest sister, Pat, remembers. 'He was funny, good-looking – and certainly didn't have any ego problems.'

Dave was a player, easily able to charm women, and had a wild side. He smoked weed, he drank and wasn't shy to get stuck in if there was a fistfight on the go. He'd often spend the morning after the night before in the Clinton-Parkers' kitchen, with Megs feeding his hangover. Sometimes she even found herself counselling his heart-broken girlfriends at the behest of his mother.

By the age of 25, Dave was divorced with two sons and working as a saw doctor at a mill in the Weza area, east of Kokstad. Every so often he'd travel to Maritzburg to have a night on the town. One weekend in May 1988 he landed up at the Black Stag, a popular nightspot with live music. Megs was there with a group of friends. Megs and Dave ended up spending the night together. She saw him the following evening, also at the Stag, and felt a bit embarrassed. Her embarrassment turned to incredulity, then outrage, when she saw him disappear with a friend of her sister's. But that was Dave and how everyone knew him.

Months after, having moved from Weza to Karkloof, near Howick, Dave began dating one of Megs' friends. She told him Megs had mysteriously moved to Johannesburg.

★

It took Megs four months to muster the courage to tell her parents she was pregnant.

She felt she'd let the side down. It would have been easier to tell them she'd been fired. So she clammed up, refusing to say who the father was. With hindsight, she underestimated them: 'Of course they knew it was Dave because he was so often around,' she admits now. 'But here I was, pregnant and single, and Mum insisted on taking me to Welfare to research adoption options, which I had no intention of ever carrying out. I was determined that I would do this on my own.'

She didn't tell Dave at all. She knew he would find out from his mother, Margaret. 'Regrettably my insecurities never allowed me to believe that he would want me,' she says. 'While I was outgoing and social, I was not sure of myself when it came to relationships. I didn't want to make him feel trapped, and believed that my parents would never accept him. They liked Dave but didn't approve of his lifestyle. So I set out to be a single mother.'

When Gavin was about eight months old, Megs' father asked her to phone Dave. He'd lent him a CB radio and he wanted it back. Megs procrastinated, but her father asked again, and eventually − reluctantly − she picked up the phone. It had been more than a year since she'd last seen Dave. She'd stayed in Nigel with her sister and baby Gavin for five months before returning to Pietermaritzburg.

Dave said he'd sold the CB radio. Megs jokingly berated him. Then he said: 'I need to ask you something. Will you tell me the truth?'

Megs knew what was coming.

'That child you've just had − is it mine?'

She acknowledged that it was. He said they should talk about it. He was coming into town that week.

Dave met Megs at her parents' house. 'I decided I should see this child who was meant to be my son,' Dave says. 'We went upstairs to talk. Gavin was sleeping in his cot. I found it impossible to absorb that he was mine.' Megs reiterated that she didn't expect anything of him. He already had two other children he was meant to be supporting.

'I told him I expected nothing from him. And that was that − he went home.'

But six months later, she found herself unemployed and struggling to make ends meet. Her funds had dried up and she couldn't live off her parents forever. She phoned Dave and told him she needed help. He was non-committal then began avoiding her. She could never get hold of him. Her brother Geoff eventually went to see him and told him he needed to support his child, even if only temporarily, until Megs started earning. Dave didn't budge.

Next thing Megs heard through the grapevine that Dave had decided he wasn't the father of her baby. Dave says his mother, who had attended Gavin's christening, had said to him: 'That child isn't a Lotter.'

Megs was furious. 'What did they think of me? If the pregnancy itself was embarrassing, it was absolutely nothing compared with the humiliation of being told by one of your friends that the father did not think your child was his. I decided to prove it to him.'

She approached her family GP, Doctor Watson, and asked him how she could go about proving that Dave was the father. He explained that a simple blood test wouldn't suffice. It had to follow a legal course, not a medical one.

She decided to sue Dave, a decision she didn't take lightly. 'You must understand that this was extremely traumatic for me,' she says. 'But I wanted him to know I wasn't some cheap sleaze, nor would I lie to him about something like that.'

Dave thinks he had every right to question the paternity of the child: 'Megs also had an active social life. She dated other guys too, so I had to be sure the baby was mine.'

Megs found herself a lawyer.

Nowadays, Richard Stretch is the senior partner at Lister & Lister. Back then, he was the company rookie, dealing with routine cases – and this one certainly seemed to fit the bill. Megs said the child could only have been conceived with Dave.

Blood tests would decide it.

★

On 21 November 1990, Richard Stretch received the results of Megs', Dave's and Gavin's blood tests in the post. He couldn't believe what he was reading.

> The HLA and PGM1 types of Gavin Clinton-Parker are such that he must have received from his biological mother either factor B5 or B7 in the HLA system, and factor 1A in the PGM1 system. Margaret Clinton-Parker does not possess any of these factors. It is therefore not possible for her to be the biological mother of Gavin.

Nor was it possible for Dave to be Gavin's father.

> The putative father in this case (Dave Lotter) is excluded as the biological father of the child Gavin as he also does not possess either factor B5 or B7, one of which must have been contributed by the child's biological father.

Richard Stretch's immediate thought was that Megs was some kind of con artist. 'I got a helluva fright,' he confesses. 'I thought Megs must be committing fraud to get maintenance … it didn't occur to me at first that someone could have swapped the babies.'

He decided to hand the results to his senior partner, Richard Lister, who knew Megs personally, and asked him if he could tell her. He himself just couldn't. Richard Lister phoned Megs and told her he needed to see her urgently. She knew it had to be about the test results and asked what the problem was.

He told her Dave wasn't the father.

She told him that wasn't possible.

'You need to come and see me,' he said. 'It's complicated.'

★

Richard Lister paced around his office as he repeated to Megs: 'He's not the father.'

Megs sat staring at him. She knew Richard well. He'd been a regular at the photographic studio where she'd worked, always needing printing done in a hurry for a case or an insurance claim. She and a friend or her sister Pat had looked after his house on occasion when he went on holiday. They'd been house sitting for him in 1988 when Pat had noticed Megs throwing up every morning and realised she was pregnant.

Now he was telling her something that made no sense.

'What do you mean?' Megs gasped. 'It's impossible.'

'Well … I got the test's results back and he's not the father. But it's more complicated than that … um …

He was holding a sheet of paper in his hand, but seemed unable to articulate what was on it.

Megs reached out for it: 'Let me read it then.'

He hesitantly handed it over.

Megs recalls: 'And that's how I found out. Boom! It was like I had been stabbed. My hair literally stood on end. I walked out of Lister & Lister and went down the road to the photo shop where a dear friend still worked. I collapsed on the floor at the back of the shop. It was as if I had passed out from shock. Then I cried. I cried for the child I had and the child I didn't have. I knew without a shadow of a doubt my life had changed forever.'

The swap could only have happened at birth, so Richard Stretch set about trying to find out who else had been in the maternity ward at the Nigel Hospital on 17 February 1989. Staff checked the records. They phoned back to say there'd only been one other mother there whose baby had been born on the same day. They'd be informing Sandy Dawkins that she needed to come in for a blood test.

★

Sandy was at work when a Sister Mostert called from the hospital.

She recalls the phone call: 'The sister asked if I'd had a baby boy on the 17th of February 1989, and to bring him in – come for an interview and blood tests. I asked who was demanding the tests, and why, and she said that all they knew was that a woman by the name of Clinton-Parker was requesting the tests and there might have been a baby swap.'

Sandy remembered Megs immediately. Except for one other woman, who left with her baby the day after they'd arrived, they'd been the only patients in the maternity ward. They'd shared sandwiches and a flask of coffee Megs' sister Kit had brought from home. They'd laughed a lot, smoked outside together and fed their babies together.

'Megs asked me to keep an eye on Gavin while she ran to the nursery,' Sandy recalled. 'I agreed and stood looking at him and wondered about his looks. He had dark hair and so did Megs … then she came back and when the boys went to sleep we left the ward to enjoy a cigarette and chat.'

A shocked Sandy left work at Standard Bank in the Johannesburg city centre to fetch Robin from day-care. When she'd dropped him off that morning he'd been hers. Now she didn't know. She'd recently split from Jeff, whom she'd believed to be Robin's father. She was pregnant with their second child.

Jeff remembers getting a phone call from Sandy's supervisor at work, a man he'd been at school with. It was a terrible blow: 'I literally had a mini-stroke I was so shocked. I had to go straight to the doctor. Doctor Uys, the same doctor who delivered our baby. He called it a "terrestrial stroke" and gave me a prescription for medicine that cost 65 cents! Then I went to see Sandy and Robin – my cute boy with his blue eyes and blonde hair.'

Sandy was beside herself. Even though Jeff and she had separated, he and Robin were nuts about each other. They didn't know what to do except hold tight onto their child.

Once they'd calmed down, Jeff tried to find out more. He remembers it all clearly: 'I went to the Nigel Hospital and heard from them that the other boy's name was Clinton Parker. I battled to determine who these people were, whose child we had. I thought the surname was Parker, first name Clinton.'

When he tried to get hold of the 'Parkers' from Pietermaritzburg, Telkom directory inquiries for some reason put him through to the local fire station. Staff there told him they knew a Peter Clinton-Parker, an engineer with the Pietermaritzburg

City Council. He turned out to be Megs' father.

'I spoke to his wife Joan, Megs' mother,' Jeff relates, 'and after work the next afternoon, I hopped onto my motorbike. It was a 1300 Kawasaki that Robin just loved. I would lift him round the garden on it. I got to Pietermaritzburg at eight that night, it was raining cats and dogs and I was soaked. I told Peter and Joan that as far as I was concerned Robin was my child, not Gavin. Joan was a great lady. I came to admire her over the years. She immediately reassured me that she would not expect us to give Robin back.'

Jeff felt no emotions when he saw his biological son for the first time. Compared to Robin, he thought he was spoilt, 'a very demanding child. I felt nothing when I saw him. I had bonded with Robin.'

On 11 December Sandy, Jeff and Robin went to the SA Medical Institute in Braamfontein to have blood tests. For Jeff, it was a continuation of the nightmare:

'They stuck a needle in Robin's neck, I'm not sure why they needed to take blood from there. Maybe his other veins were too small. He cried and I got cross because they hurt my boy.'

A few days before Christmas 1990, the confirmation finally arrived:

SOUTH AFRICAN INSTITUTE FOR MEDI-
CAL RESEARCH: IMMUNOHAEMATOLOGY
DEPARTMENT

CONCLUSIONS: There are contra-indications to the laws of theoretical expectancy in these findings, in that:
  All blood group factors arise by inheritance. It is

not possible for a human being to possess a blood group factor if neither parent possesses it. The child ROBIN possesses the A factor of the ABO system and the E factor of the Rh system. Neither Sandra Dawkins nor Jeffrey Parsons possess this factor. Also the blood group of Jeffrey Parsons is such that he must pass on to all his offspring the C factor. The child does not possess this factor. It is not possible for Robin to be born out of a union of these two adults.

Gavin Clinton-Parker and Robin Dawkins had been switched and were living each other's lives.

But they were lives that had to go on. One evening Megs and her mother Joan took Gavin to a work Christmas party. In the lift a colleague looked at Gavin and remarked, 'Isn't he a chip off the old block?' He couldn't understand why she and Joan started laughing.

Most of the time there was nothing to laugh about. Megs was on treatment for stress and shock. She began eating less and drinking more, chain smoking. She developed suppurating abscesses in her ears: 'I had these huge pink cauliflower ears … the pain was excruciating. I'd wake up with gunge on my pillow and my hair. I went on three courses of antibiotics. Painkillers seemed to have no effect.'

★

Megs respected that gut-feel must have told Dave Lotter that Gavin wasn't his. Nonetheless Dave was still part of the dilemma she found herself in. Joan phoned his mother, Margaret, and Megs' sister Pat took on the job of phoning Dave, telling them they needed to meet. Margaret's first thought was that the test results had revealed some kind of an illness. She was speechless when she heard the real reason.

Dave didn't really see how it was his problem. He was about to announce his engagement to his second wife. 'I knew Megs was having a rough time,' he conceded, 'but I wasn't in a position to call the shots. I didn't know anything about the other child and hadn't been given confirmation that I was anyone's father.'

Megs partly blamed him for the heart-breaking dilemma she found herself in: 'If he'd come out with it right from the start, when he first saw Gavin, that he didn't think Gavin was his, things might've worked out entirely differently. Instead we found out when the boys were toddlers.'

Megs says Dave was uninterested when she told him that they had located the boy who could be his son.

'I want to stay out of it' was all he would say.

Dave didn't think he owed Megs anything: 'I hadn't been in-cluded from the start and was only roped in after she'd had the child. Obviously this latest news that he was the wrong child must've been a helluva slap in the face for her. Here she was trying to prove that I was the kid's father and the whole thing backfires.'

Megs couldn't understand his reasoning. She'd still given birth to his child. She developed a deep resentment towards Dave, who was not even prepared to provide emotional support, it seemed. She often wonders how her life would have been had she not been so determined to get even with him. 'Humiliation is a powerful antidote for any positive feelings. And that humiliation has stayed with me,' she says. 'I am still not comfortable talking about the pregnancy or the blood tests because of it. As it turned out, I opened a can of worms that would affect everyone.'

★

In 1996, Sandy Dawkins spoke out to *60 Minutes.* 'Why did she have to do this and disrupt everyone's lives?' she protested. 'If it was me, I would've probably kept the whole thing quiet and gotten on with it.'

Jeffrey Parsons, now in his late sixties, agrees. 'I think of Robin often and to this day I consider him my son, blood ties or not,' he says. 'It would have been better not knowing.'

But they did know. Jeff traced Dave's family and spoke to Margaret.

'I wanted to know who Robin's biological father was,' he confesses. 'I had a conversation with Dave's mother and told her Robin was a well-behaved boy and that I would send photographs.'

★

While Jeff had little desire to bond with Gavin, Megs was torn between wanting to protect the child she had and her desire to see the one she didn't have. She began obsessing about Robin.

She never felt like eating, so didn't. But drinking helped dull the pain. One evening, after a few glasses of wine and no food, she had an argument with her parents and drove off in tears with 20-month-old Gavin strapped in the back seat. While fumbling to light a cigarette she lost control of the car and crashed into a fire hydrant.

'There was water everywhere,' she remembers. 'Luckily I was just badly bruised and Gav wasn't hurt, although he got a helluva fright. But it made me pull myself together. I never drove after drinking again.'

Megs spent a long session with her GP. She told him that she believed God equipped people to deal with whatever they had the mental ability to cope with, no matter how difficult or impossible it seemed.

Joan phoned Sandy and suggested that they meet.

Megs had already had weeks to adjust, but Sandy was still trying to digest the shocking news. She was slightly miffed by Joan's tone: 'She said, *Aren't you interested in seeing the child you gave birth to?* I told her quite frankly, I wasn't. I was scared.'

But she spoke to Jeff and he agreed he'd take her to Maritzburg when it was convenient work-wise. This vague arrangement didn't suit Megs, now desperate to meet her biological son.

Sandy began to feel bullied: 'Megs carried on and on,' she recalls, 'and by the fourth phone call started threatening me with lawyers and a court order. I told her straight I didn't have the money for the trip. Next thing I knew Joan had bought two tickets and I was on a six-hour bus trip with a two-year-old who couldn't sit still and who had no clue that I wasn't his mother.'

The last time Megs had seen Sandy — and her biological son — was in hospital 23 months before.

She had invited Sandy's mother to come too so that she wouldn't feel she was among strangers, but Sandy came alone. Megs remembers thinking it was brave of her to leave her comfort zone.

They were the last off the bus. Robin walked slightly in front of Sandy, holding her hand.

Sandy remembers not wanting to get off the bus at all. 'I often wonder how different things would've been had we just stayed on the bus and gone back home.'

Megs had never even seen a picture of Robin. When she caught sight of him there was no turning back.

She had no doubt he was hers. She gave him a hug and quickly let go.

She would later tell *60 Minutes*: 'When I first saw Robin, when he got off that bus, I actually produced milk – that's how strong the maternal instinct was. After not feeding Gavin for a year, I produced milk as if I'd almost just given birth. That's how strong the pull was, and you can't just let that go. I was never going to let go.'

They went for more blood tests, which only confirmed what they already knew.

THE NATAL BLOOD TRANSFUSION SERVICE

Dear Ms Clinton-Parker
You would not be excluded as the natural mother of the child Robin and Sandra Dawkins would not be excluded as the natural mother of Gavin.

The rest of their week together was spent getting to know the little boys they'd carried for nine months, but never seen again. Even though he was only two, Megs noticed Clinton-Parker characteristics in Robin and saw similarities between Gavin and Sandy. The way Robin stood sometimes reminded Megs of her father.

Pat, who'd always thought Gavin looked a bit like her, saw echoes of Dave in Robin's outgoing and mischievous manner.

14

In Gavin, Sandy saw a miniature Jeff: 'Even the way he walked … small steps with a bit of a bum waggle, more pronounced when he was cross about something.'

The toddlers got on well, but Sandy felt tired and strained during the visit, staying with Megs in her parents' big old house. To her mind, it was as if they were watching her to see if she was good enough to bring up their child.

At the end of the week, a tearful Megs put her son back on the bus with a relieved Sandy. 'It was terrible when he left,' she told Richard Carleton on *60 Minutes,* 'like having your whole womb taken away.'

The following month they celebrated the boys' second birthdays together and Jeff drove down with Sandy, Robin, and Sandy's mother, Kay. They all stayed with the Clinton-Parkers.

Pictures show skinny Robin and chubby Gavin bathing together, drinking their bottles, riding their plastic scooters – like blood brothers. The day after their birthday party they took the boys to Durban, Robin's first trip to the beach. There's a photograph of a visibly pregnant Sandy feeding pigeons; the boys chasing them in other pictures. Megs felt better than she had in months. 'It was a day that made me so happy,' she recalled. 'I really thought things would work out if we could just keep meeting up.'

They tried. Megs and Gavin travelled to Johannesburg by bus and Jeff picked them up from the Heidelberg Railway Station. They visited grandmother Kay and Jeff's sister Jenny, who was close to Robin.

Megs concedes that they were essentially good people. But nothing about the life into which her biological son had mistakenly been placed made her feel at ease. Everyone in Sandy's family seemed to have left school before finishing or to have had an illegitimate child. And Sandy had another one on the way. In Megs' family, illegitimacy was totally unacceptable. She was the only unmarried parent in the Clinton-Parker clan.

★

At Lister & Lister, Richard Stretch's work wasn't over. He now had an entirely different maintenance issue on his hands. His client, Megs, needed help in bringing up her son, but couldn't sue Jeff Parsons, because he was already supporting Robin. Although, says Jeff, it didn't stop Megs trying: 'I got a letter from her after I'd remarried, demanding maintenance for Gavin. To make matters worse, she got her sister in Nigel to give the letter to Audrey, my wife. I had to again explain that I was maintaining Robin.'

Megs felt Sandy should sue Dave for maintenance, so that she could indirectly get some monetary support for Gavin, via Sandy. They even drew up a draft agreement:

> 7.1 Sandy agrees to pursue a claim for maintenance against Dave Lotter and upon successful finalization of such a claim she agrees to make payment to Megs of the amount paid by Lotter for the maintenance and support of Gavin, Dave Lotter being the natural father of the child in Sandy's care.

Sandy never signed the agreement, which she later said was cooked up by the Clinton-Parkers, although Megs recalls her being fine with it at the time. They'd sat and discussed it with

16

Richard Stretch and decided suing each other's partners was the only way for both of them to get maintenance for their children. Sandy says she actually thought it was ridiculous that she should sue someone she 'didn't know from Adam' and that Megs was doing it just to spite Dave.

By this time Dave had moved to Malawi. He says the first he heard he was expected to pay maintenance was after the court case, when someone he knew alerted him after reading *Fair Lady* magazine. Sue Grant-Marshall's article was called 'A Never-ending Story'.

> Hidden behind the screaming headlines lies the true tragedy of baby-swap mothers Megs Clinton-Parker and Sandy Dawkins. For the rest of their lives they will question a decision they made in 1991 ... Neither they nor their families will ever fully escape the consequences of that swap.

Four pages on:

> Robin's biological father Dave Lotter, who is married and living in Malawi, has made no attempt to see him or pay maintenance.

Dave says he hadn't had any communication with anybody saying he was officially the father of a boy called Robin Dawkins. 'No one ever came to me with a piece of paper,' he says. 'Now I had my two young sons, to whom I was a hero, asking me what I'd done. I had to explain to them that yes, I did once sleep with Megs, but that she'd ended up with the wrong child and I had no idea whether the other one was mine or not.

'I guess I was hoping that I wasn't the father, because one doesn't want children out of marriage. Anyway, they soon got so involved in suing the hospital that no one ever got hold of me. They just spoke to journalists about me, who of course never bothered to ask my opinion.'

Sandy says she would certainly have asked Dave's opinion given the chance, but that Megs steadfastly refused to give her his contact details, even when she was expected to extract maintenance from him. Megs doesn't recall Sandy ever asking.

Back in Pietermaritzburg, Richard Stretch concentrated his efforts on making the state pay – in this case, the Transvaal Provincial Administration, under whose jurisdiction the Nigel Hospital fell. Proving negligence on the part of the hospital wouldn't be tricky, but proving that the trauma and shock of the discovery had impacted on Megs and Sandy mentally and physically was going to be precedent setting.

In a case that was to kick-start his career, Richard began work.

The Case

10 April 1991

Dear Megs

DAMAGES CLAIM: NIGEL HOSPITAL

Further to our telecon of yesterday we confirm that we are now to proceed against the Transvaal Provincial Administration.

In this regard, the matter has already been referred to the State Attorney, Transvaal, and we are in contact with him.

Yours faithfully

Richard Stretch
Lister & Lister

Although warned that the chances of winning a case were remote, Megs' plight had crept under Richard's skin. He'd recently had a daughter and hadn't let her out of his sight until she'd been tagged 'Baby Stretch' by the nurses.

'This was a tragedy,' he says, 'and I learned in Roman Law that "Where there's a wrong, there's a remedy." The problem was that there were no physical manifestations of this tragedy: only emotional scars. But just because the law couldn't see their injuries, didn't mean there weren't any. Nonetheless, I foresaw that quantifying damages would be tricky.'

As the attorney, Richard had to find a legal team and manage the finances. Except he could find neither. It was a case few would touch. Everybody took it for granted it would fail. And as single working mothers, Megs and Sandy couldn't fund a costly court case.

Richard applied for legal aid. They hummed and hawed, saying it was risky – could he first get the backing of senior counsel?

He approached an advocate in Durban, who sent him a three-page opinion, basically telling him to abandon the case. Richard began to despair.

'I needed someone to think out-of-the-box and no one was prepared to do that … it was 1991, South Africa was still very conservative. There wasn't a progressive Child Care Act; everything was vastly different. Today, just in terms of our Constitution we would have had a case.'

He eventually found his out-of-the-box thinker – Pietermaritzburg senior advocate Con Hartzenberg, admitted to the bar in 1978, with plenty of experience in civil cases. He would later go on to represent Adri Naude, whose ex-boyfriend Lawrie Fraser in 1997 challenged her right to give up their baby for adoption.

Today Hartzenberg has retired from active practice at the bar and counts these two cases as among the most memorable of his 37-year career.

'I enjoyed cases where there wasn't a precedent,' he explains. 'My philosophy was that if a client had a legitimate case he or she had a right to have that case presented in court in the best possible way. I believed the ladies, Ms Clinton-Parker and Ms Dawkins, had suffered an injustice that needed to be redressed. Look, you never know if you will win, but I thought they had a sound cause and a morally just cause that I could take forward for them. I wasn't one to shy away from a challenge.'

Sandy Sarantos, the junior advocate on the team, is less formal: 'Excuse my French, but Con had heavy balls — he wasn't scared of anything. He was a very good advocate — clever and hard-working. Without a guy of his calibre we would not have succeeded.'

Looking back, Sarantos remembers at times wondering what on earth they were doing. The law was substantially against them, there was a distinct lack of financial wherewithal to get the matter to court and there were the logistical difficulties of shuttling between Johannesburg and Pietermaritzburg. They were representing people who couldn't finance the litigation. There was an understandable reluctance from other lawyers to get involved in a case like this. There was a risk they might never get paid.

With Con Hartzenberg prepared to take the risk and both Sandy Sarantos and Richard aware that a high-profile case like this would be good for their young careers, they began looking for funding.

22 November 1991

Dear Megs

YOURSELF AND MS DAWKINS/TRANSVAAL PROVINCIAL ADMINISTRATION

We are pleased to advise that we have approached Lawyers for Human Rights with a view to them funding the litigation proposed against the Transvaal Provincial Administration.

In this regard a formal application has been made and writer has been in telephonic contact with Ms A Skelton. She advises she has in turn spoken to the head of the Funding Department who has indicated that funds should be forthcoming...

Yours faithfully

Richard Stretch
Lister & Lister

Although Megs and Sandy had 'suffered an infringement of their fundamental rights to mental well being at the hands of a state institution that hadn't exercised elementary precautions' there were no local cases in which similar facts had been presented. Their legal team needed to prove to the court that the brain and the nervous system were as much part of the physical body as an arm or a leg.

They decided their best bet as a precedent was a 1973 case, Bester v Commercial Union, in which the judge held that 'there was no reason in our law why somebody who, as the result of a negligent act of another, has suffered psychiatric injury ... should not be entitled to compensation...'.

In the Bester case, an 11-year-old boy had witnessed a car colliding with and killing his brother, aged six. The older boy was deeply traumatised.

His father sued the insurance company of the driver of the vehicle. The driver's negligence hadn't been disputed. It was held on appeal that the father was entitled to compensation, on his older son's behalf, for the change in personality that the child had sustained.

The Judge, JA Botha, pointed out that damages were regularly awarded for shock, pain and suffering, but only when accompanied by physical injury. His conclusion was that 'to deny a victim compensation purely on the basis that the shock and consequential harm were not allied to a physical injury cannot be defended logically'.

Although the facts of Megs' and Sandy's case would be precedent setting, it was this principle, says Con Hartzenberg, which had to be 'pulled through' – that the plaintiffs had suffered psychiatric injury, not just emotional shock.

'This was not a straightforward case,' he says. 'We needed to demonstrate to the court that their psychiatric injury had physical manifestations; be it loss of appetite, insomnia, an inability to concentrate. We had to prove the extent of their mental turmoil and anxiety.'

★

For the next year, Megs and Sandy would undergo extensive psycho-
metric testing. Experts had to examine the impact the trauma
of the discovery had had on them. By doing this, they could
determine the cost of future care – how much counselling and
psychiatric treatment they would need until the boys were adults.

Megs found the hours of what seemed like interrogation stress-
ful. She felt pressurised into appearing to be deeply emotionally
affected by the swap, when most of the time she just felt dead and
expressionless.

The state's expert, Anne-Marie Wentzel, would later state in
her preliminary psychological report: 'emotionally Ms Clinton-
Parker seems to be lifeless'.

The experts were all based in Johannesburg or Pretoria, which
meant a trek for Megs. Sometimes she had to take Gavin with her
so that their relationship could be assessed.

'One month I went up three times,' she remembers. 'I would
get on the late-night bus from Maritzburg and arrive in Jo'burg
in the morning. It was draining – on the senses and the pocket. I
had to borrow money from my parents to afford the to-ing and
fro-ing.'

Funds collected to finance the case were used to pay the experts. They couldn't be hired on a contingency basis. Con was
adamant about this: 'I don't get involved in a case if the experts
are only paid if the case is won. That's asking for trouble. It will
put your experts in a situation where they are no longer impartial
or independent. They have to be honest and frank if the outcome
of the case is dependent on their evidence.'

Clinical psychologist Jayni Bloch wrote after a session with Megs and Gavin:

> At the moment Margaret feels she cannot accept or confront her present situation. She feels degraded and let down. Since discovering the swap of the babies she has been suffering ear ache and ear abscesses, six times.
>
> She has also gained weight, then lost 36kg over six months in the past year. She has developed boils on her legs.
>
> She has poor concentration and can no longer cope with her UNISA B.Com studies.
>
> She is obsessed about the two boys and feels help-less, powerless and without rights.
>
> She feels uncertain and insecure about the future and is not able to make any plans. There are too many confusing legal and practical implications for her to handle.
>
> She experiences extreme anger particularly towards Sandra, whom she feels is not a good enough mother and also towards the fathers of the boys whom she feels have disowned their responsibilities.

Of Gavin, the report says:

> Gavin was relaxed and organized. He drew pictures on his own while his mother spoke to me. He was con-cerned about her at times, but settled down quickly. He is capable of keeping himself busy. He is not very

talkative. He answers: 'I don't know' to any questions put to him. His drawings are colourful and friendly.

Sandy saw Jayni Bloch too: sometimes on her own, once with Jeff, several times with Robin. The report says she suffered tremendous tension and anxiety:

> She feels confused and vulnerable and that her ordinary daily life has been disturbed and disrupted with an unsolvable problem.
>
> She loves her son Robin whom she has brought up so far and given all her love and care, but she feels guilt, curiosity and longing for her biological son.
>
> The question that haunts her is which son she should feel responsible to, her biological son or the one she cared for up to the present and bonded with completely?
>
> The bond between Sandra and Robin is strong and healthy. He is comfortable with her and responds with spontaneity and confidence. Eye and physical contact is healthy. Their verbal communication is warm and relaxed.
>
> Jeffrey Parsons is concerned about Robin. He too relates well to Robin, who calls him Daddy. Robin has fully accepted Jeffrey as his father and Sandra as his mother. He has also adapted to their physical circumstances, of not living together as a married couple. He has regular meaningful contact with Jeffrey and looks forward to visiting him.

Both women, it was concluded, showed signs of a 'psychosomatic syndrome, with psychological features affecting their physical condition'. Megs had eating issues; Sandy had sleeping issues. Both were often close to tears; both were distracted and had mood swings.

Another assessment described Sandy as having symptoms of a depressive disorder, including 'a significant weight loss, depressed mood, insomnia, incapacity at work …'

Sandy had never been depressed in her life. Now suddenly she felt weighed down. At work she was given one written warning after the other and eventually fired, she says, because of an inability to concentrate.

'Until the 30th of November 1990 I had been happy, able to support my son and myself on my salary and I was at work every day. Suddenly I was moody and my behaviour erratic. No one at work seemed willing to put themselves in my shoes. I cried for the smallest thing, I became anti-social … I lacked the stamina to go on as I did before. I burst into tears for the smallest things. I often became angry beyond expression when I looked at Robin. There was no joy in my life any more.'

Megs didn't know if what she was doing was best for the children. She feared that Robin would, as he got older, not understand her reasoning for leaving him in Sandy's care, that he might turn around and say: 'I am your real son, why didn't you want me?'

She worried that she might disappoint her family by keeping Gavin and not taking Robin, who resembled her father. She developed chest pains and was short of breath, not aided by her cigarette intake, which had doubled to 40 a day. Her weight continued fluctuating.

One report read: 'Early problems materialized with excessive eating. It was a period of recognizing the fact that the swap had occurred and the lifelong consequences of it.'

Sandy was booked into a clinic for sleep therapy. She was diagnosed as having a chemical imbalance, caused by intense stress.

'My life just went to pieces,' she says. 'I didn't bother about my appearance. I became irrational. I began resenting Megs for not having had her baby in Natal. Why did she have to come and have it in the same hospital as me just to avoid embarrassment? She should have just stayed where she was. No lives would've been thrown into chaos then, would they?'

The experts who assessed Megs and Sandy found that their stress was manifold.

> Megs' presentation contains most features of post-traumatic stress disorder. The primary difference is that the stress stimulus is not a single isolated incident, but an ongoing stress situation, which has little hope of terminating completely.
>
> Continued psychotherapy is essential for Sandra until she has learned to accept and live with the situation. Psychotherapy may be required for Robin in the future.

★

Compounding Megs' anxiety was that a court might prompt questions about the legal status of the boys.

'The one burning issue surrounding the trial was the possibility that the status of the children would be questioned,' she says.

'While it may not have been the focus, the possibility could not be ruled out and we had to prepare for it. I did not believe that the court would want us to swap the children back. I was more concerned that the courts would not approve of them hanging in limbo and would refer us to the family court to formalise their adoption.'

It annoyed her that one of the state experts, Anne-Marie Wentzel, persisted in questioning her about the possibility of switching back, or adopting Gavin.

'She was really pushy when it came to engaging with the children, especially Gavin who did not have an understanding of the matter and whom my family and I planned to gradually wean into the knowledge of the switch. At one stage I had to tell her to back off, as Gavin got very upset.'

Anne-Marie Wentzel wrote in one of her reports:

> Ms Clinton-Parker is highly concerned that my involvement in the matter might cause her to be forced to give up her child, Gavin. She is also highly concerned that an officer of the court might take it upon him or herself to recommend that the children be swapped. When this possibility was discussed, Ms Clinton-Parker became like a caged animal – not only frightened, but also threatened, fighting for her child.

Megs told Anne-Marie Wentzel that 'only a bus' stood between her and her children, meaning, wrote Wentzel, that 'she fantasises that Ms Dawkins would die and she would be given both children'.

Megs doesn't remember saying this, but knows she decided

soon after meeting Sandy and after seeing the environment in which Robin was growing up – the frequent moves, on/off relationships and irregular income – that they were not suitable to bringing up a child. Her child.

'It was extremely traumatic to decide whether to leave my natural son in that environment because he didn't know any better, or to place the child I loved as my own into an environment in which he could not possibly survive …'

'I can't see beyond getting both kids,' she wrote. 'I want both to live with me, but will settle for Robin living with Sandy provided I see him regularly, he gets the same educational opportunities I provide for Gavin and that he is properly cared for, i.e. staying with Sandy and not her family, has a house, is well fed and clothed.'

Sandy still resents Megs' views about her family.

'I come from a hard-working family,' she says indignantly. 'My Dad was a boilermaker, Mom a hairdresser and both of them worked after hours to provide the best for my sister and me. Dad passed away when Robin was six months and 11 days old, so he never got to find out about the dreadful mistake. Dad had provided for my mom, so she gave up work after he died and she looked after Robin and saw to his every need. Then he turned out to be a total stranger, which turned our worlds upside down.'

Although she found it difficult to accept that she had cared for someone else's child without knowing it, she feared losing him. She had nightmares about Megs arriving at her door unannounced and taking Robin. The basis of her fear, she says, was that shortly after the switch was discovered, Megs had expressly stated that 'should anything ever happen to Gavin, you can be quite sure I will take Robin'.

Advocate Con Hartzenberg, oblivious to the underlying tensions between the two mothers, had his own view. A view he never expressed because it simply wasn't relevant to the case:

'If you separate a dairy cow and her calf shortly after birth and prevent them from nursing – as often happens – and then reunite them with 20 other cows and new-born calves, they will find their mothers. The instinct is that strong. The boys should have been switched back immediately the mistake was discovered. Instinct would have taken over. Children are resilient, it is the mothers who would suffer most.'

And it was this suffering that he would set out to prove in court.

When the expert reports landed on Richard Stretch's desk, he realised they had enough to win the case.

Megs and Sandy were so emotionally traumatised that it turned out to be the easiest thing in the world to prove.

In Court

The summons was issued on 9 November 1992. On the advice of their lawyers, Megs and Sandy sued the Transvaal Provincial Administration for R138 325 each. Based on their experts' reports, R50 000 was for emotional shock, R7 319 for psychotherapy and R81 006 for travelling expenses between Nigel and Pietermaritzburg to visit their sons every second month for the next 17 years — until the boys were 21.

In papers before the court, Megs and Sandy blamed staff at the Nigel Hospital for failing to take precautions to ensure the children weren't switched. Their outrage was translated into unemotional legalese.

> They allowed the two minor children to become confused with one another in such a manner as to make it impossible to identify the child of each respective parent and/or inadvertently switched the one child for the other without taking the necessary and reasonable precautions to prevent such a switch from taking place...

In the Defendant's Plea, received in late January 1993, the state denied there'd been negligence on the part of the provincial hospital, or that systems had been inadequate, or that someone in the system had been remiss. The state asked that the claim be dismissed with costs.

This denial of negligence was tactical and completely normal, says Advocate Con Hartzenberg. The adversary was required to prove his or her case.

Hartzenberg explains: 'Sometimes it happens that the party who makes the allegation is unable to find sufficient evidence to prove the allegation for whatever reason — be it inept lawyers, or a lack of funding to employ competent expert witnesses. Perhaps the state and its legal team thought we would stumble over our own feet, or would not be able to engage sound experts.'

There was to be no stumbling. The plaintiff's legal team swung into action. They subpoenaed Megs' and Sandy's admission documents from the hospital — in which the institution had undertaken to exercise 'due and proper care' — and the medical records. This kind of paperwork is vital in negligence cases, says Hartzenberg. If left too long, it can disappear, or get tampered with. He knew from past experience they had to get onto it immediately: 'Once you get your hands on those documents, you can follow up with your client about what's in those records. It's one thing listening to your client, but those records might paint a completely different picture.'

If there was a substantial material difference in Megs' and Sandy's versions, the case couldn't proceed. They compiled detailed statements, Sandy's in longhand, Megs' typed.

There was nothing to dispute: the boys had been born a few hours apart and their mothers had identified them in the hospital nursery by the tags on their wrists and ankles. They never saw each other again until after the switch was discovered 18 months later. It could only have happened at the hospital.

Megs listed her legal and medical expenses and her travel costs, so far paid by her parents. She wrote about the cost of replacing her wardrobe from a size 42 to 32; the burden of having had no maintenance for five years because she didn't know which father to sue; the dozens of phone calls and the trips to see Robin in Johannesburg.

'My feelings have been too controlled, too everything for too long,' she vented in a letter to Richard Stretch. 'There's too much anger, too much frustration, too much stress, too many emotional feelings of despair and outrage for there not to be some form of release at some stage. I fear the witness box where this is all to be tested. Let's hope that this is not where the eruption takes place.'

Both women, remembers Hartzenberg, were at a loss as to how to cope with the situation and were profoundly troubled. There was certainly no need for dramatised dress rehearsals of what might play out in court. 'They were shocked, bewildered and sad – and that came across in all our pre-trial consultations,' he says.

Sandy wrote: 'I trust in the Almighty that the future will turn out the right way for each and everyone involved, particularly the two boys who have grown up in the "wrong" homes, but have never been more loved.'

★

The trial date was set for Friday 26 August 1994, at a time when politics in South Africa was in the throes of fundamental change:

34

Nelson Mandela had been in office for 100 days, the last of the UN sanctions had been lifted, South Africa had been accepted back in the Commonwealth, capital punishment was set to be abolished, Dimitri Tsafendas had been released from prison.

Yet two little boys who had been switched at birth made headlines:

BABY SWAP: NO PRECEDENT FOR CLAIM

LANDMARK CASE WILL BE THE FIRST OF ITS KIND TO BE HEARD BEFORE SOUTH AFRICAN COURTS...

...THREATENS TO DEVELOP INTO ONE OF THE MOST DRAMATIC COURT BATTLES THE COUNTRY HAS SEEN...

It was Richard Stretch's first high-profile case and he found the publicity almost overwhelming. He felt intimidated by the state's big guns. Even the experienced Con Hartzenberg felt at times that they were up against it.

'It's always a huge learning curve, no matter how many cases you've done, you have to try to be ahead of that curve all the time and not overlook important things,' he reflects. 'But we certainly did not perceive ourselves as being the small fry from Natal. We were confident of our case. And once the state realised we were on top of our game, they conceded negligence. But of course, they tried to employ strategies to delay and frustrate adjudication of the claims. This is not uncommon in litigious matters.'

High Court Rule 37 requires a pre-trial conference, attended by legal representatives of both parties. It's a way of avoiding time-wasting in court on issues that aren't in dispute. It can, in some cases, result in a settlement.

To this day, Richard is convinced there was an attempt by the state to exclude him from consultations. He had arranged to meet his experts – Jayni Bloch and Dr David Shevel – both of whom had been subpoenaed, at court on the Friday. But neither of them pitched. Instead, at the pre-trial conference, he was furnished with a copy of the minutes of a meeting his experts and the state's had had the night before.

Apart from having reached agreement on the signs and symptoms present in both women, which all experts had admitted were complex with many variables, it appeared they'd also decided on the treatment Megs and Sandy would receive and how long it would last.

Richard had known nothing about these discussions, during which, he was told by Jayni Bloch, she and Dr Shevel had been asked to leave the room while the state's experts made telephonic contact with the state's junior counsel, Advocate LJ van der Merwe.

This was highly irregular, without counsel for the plaintiffs being in attendance too. On emerging, Jayni Bloch told him, state expert Anne-Marie Wentzel announced that the entire matter had been settled. So the state's experts, in phone contact with the defence advocate, had been in on the Plaintiffs' treatment regime without their legal representative being informed and without being there to negotiate a settlement, if there was to be one.

Richard was livid. 'We are dismayed at what transpired at the meeting of the expert witnesses,' he wrote to the State Attorney.

'The entire pre-trial conference took place in the belief that the panel of experts had held a meaningful conference without being subject to influence by or on behalf of either the Plaintiffs or the Defendant, which clearly in these circumstances had not happened.'

There was no way, said Richard, that his clients would accept the treatment, cost and timeframes prescribed by the state experts, who had written up the minutes and presented them to the others for signature as if all had been settled. He suggested another meeting, this time in the presence of Megs' and Sandy's counsel.

But, in what felt like the ultimate dirty trick, the state was granted a postponement to August 1995.

Megs and Sandy were hugely disheartened – they would have to wait another year for justice. It just seemed useless and endless, Sandy said. They wanted to get to court and make them pay for this horrific mistake. Not that it would change matters.

Con Hartzenberg was pragmatic, seeing it as nothing more than a procedural obstacle, a diversion. 'It's fairly typical, part of brinkmanship and strategy,' he explains. 'Medical negligence cases are no exception. There will be a simple amendment to a pleading then suddenly the other side needs time to investigate. The defendants hope that fatigue will set in and both plaintiffs and the legal representatives will get sick and tired of it and just walk away. It does happen. It's inherent in this type of litigation ... Postponements are endemic; they happen very frequently and serve to up levels of frustration and anger. You just have to cope with them and be patient. Court systems are not efficient. Latterly, they are showing a level of dysfunction that is rather alarming.'

Megs felt far more emotional about the situation. 'It was with some surprise and dismay that I discovered the postponement of the trial after three and a half years of waiting,' she wrote. 'Now we must wait another year, a year which will only serve to worsen all aspects of both our lives.'

Another year before they could even consider being compensated. Until then, they'd have to bear the cost of therapy and counselling and travel between Johannesburg and Pietermaritzburg to see their children.

'We needed proper counselling and Sandy in particular wasn't getting it,' Megs explains. 'I wanted to see Robin every holiday, but couldn't afford it.'

Robin was a gregarious child, happy to leave home to spend time with Megs. His 'sister' Jessica would accompany him. But Gavin was reluctant to visit Sandy on his own, sometimes leaving her wondering why she should share Robin if Megs didn't reciprocate. Her hurt was clear: 'I ended up watching Gavin growing up through his biological sister, Jessica. It was very difficult, seeing her and not him.'

Megs says she tried. She remembers dropping Gavin off with Sandy and Grandma Kay one weekend when she was in Johannesburg for a wedding. 'I phoned her and said: would she like to have Gavin for the night? She agreed, but phoned me in the evening, saying he wanted to be fetched. I explained I could only fetch him the next day. When I got there he was waiting at the gate with his tog bag in the one hand and his little scooter in the other. He got into the car and said he was never ever coming back. And that was that. I could hardly force him. And she never asked to have him. Ever.'

Sandy has her own perspective: 'I often wonder how much brainwashing Megs did about us. She influenced Gavin's thinking about us and then did the same to Robin. She promised him everything under the sun and he would get it.'

Richard Stretch hasn't had contact with Megs and Sandy for years, but remembers that back then, the relationship between them was tempestuous and he often felt caught in the middle. Megs would phone him complaining about Sandy not giving him access to Robin and he'd have to sort it out.

In the run-up to the second court date, he wanted the mothers to present a united front and steer clear of the media. There would be plenty of time to air their views about one another post-judgment.

He and his senior partner Richard Lister were convinced the state was keeping an eye on the situation, hoping to capitalise on tensions between the women. Megs became paranoid, especially when Lister told her not to use her home phone under any circumstances.

★

Megs had another session with Jayni Bloch in August 1995, a few weeks before the case resumed. The clinical psychological report noted:

> Session with Margaret:
> Margaret is more relaxed than last year this time. She has met John, with whom she has a relationship. This relationship has helped her to feel supported and has improved her confidence. She feels she can cope with the stress of the worries about the children better.

39

She has developed better eating habits and has not fluctuated as severely in her body weight this year. Stress still affects her sleep with nightmares and anxious thoughts. She is especially worried about losing Gavin and concerned about Robin's quality of life. Margaret feels that she will always be responsible for both the boys. She is still smoking 30 cigarettes a day.

Session with Gavin:
Gavin is in Grade One. He looked healthy and well cared for. He seemed intensely aware of Margaret's emotions and reactions. When he felt that she was comfortable, he relaxed. When she got anxious, he reacted nervously...

He drew raindrops. His wishes were to go to Disneyworld, see Roxette and fly like a bird.

The conclusion in the report dated 23 August 1994 still applies. The history during the past year has confirmed that the trauma of the swapping incident is continuing, despite personal and emotional support from a new relationship. Anxiety and depression still affect her and her child's life.

Support, guidance and therapy must be made available to Margaret and Gavin because of their crisis.

Two weeks later, on Monday, 21 August 1995, the case finally got underway: 'The matter between Clinton-Parker, Margaret Claire, Dawkins, Sandra, and The Administrator of the Province of the Transvaal' now had as the Defendant the Premier of Gauteng.

★

The practice in Johannesburg is that the allocation of a judge only gets made on the morning of a case, which makes it a bit like a lucky dip. But if a case is complicated, or unusual, as this one was, the decision is more considered. Con, Richard and Sandy Sarantos waited to hear who would be assigned. They didn't want an old-school judge wary of precedent setting, or reluctant to make the connection between physical and mental injury. They needed someone forward thinking – as Sarantos says, 'a new-age judge carrying none of the conservative baggage of the past like so many of his senior colleagues, who were not prepared to break new ground and make new law.'

In the brand new world of 1995 there was a fresh generation of judges emerging, some of them mentored by old South African judges.

Mahomed Navsa was a protégé of Transvaal Judge President Frikkie Eloff. The story went that Eloff had hand-picked Navsa onto the bench because he showed such exceptional promise. Today, Navsa sits on the Supreme Court of Appeal. Then, he was an unknown entity. He'd been appointed an acting judge in January 1995 and Richard recalls being extremely nervous about what he perceived to be Navsa's lack of experience in the hot seat. They could only hope and pray he would be sympathetic to their case, and not be put off by the overwhelming public sympathy for the plaintiffs.

There were newspaper articles every single day the trial ran, Richard remembers, and he was getting dozens of calls from journalists and even publications he'd never heard of. 'Nobody could fathom what those two mothers went through – and that was the appeal.'

Newspapers carried pictures of Megs and Sandy, together for the first time in months, both dressed in white shirts and black jackets, standing back to back, the sandstone arch and columns of the Rand Supreme Court behind them.

Richard recalls Megs smoking cigarette after cigarette outside court on that first morning. They'd decided to put the mothers on the witness stand that afternoon.

Megs was up first.

'I was extremely nervous. I was asked to state the symptoms I had as a result of the switch. I named a few and at Con Hartzenberg's request, the State Attorney accepted that I suffered the symptoms listed by the experts. I was asked how many children I had and I said "two". There was a flutter around the court, as they thought I'd had another child. Con asked me to clarify and I said: "Robin and Gavin".'

She explained how Gavin had been part of her life for two years before she realised he wasn't hers. She'd breast-fed him and given him her full-time attention for the first ten months of his life. She would never have considered giving him up. When she discovered he wasn't her natural child, she felt threatened and initially wanted to adopt him. The swap, she told the court tearfully, had affected her whole life: 'It just changed everything. It affected my work, my ability to trust people, to form relationships.'

While she had doubts about her decision not to part with Gavin, she believed it was the correct one. But she wanted to see Robin often and didn't have the financial means to do so.

Sandy, who remembers being a ball of nerves in court, described her constant depression and frequent anxiety attacks. She said she had lost ambition and wasn't prepared to make commitments. In 1992 she was off work for two weeks, in 1993 she took 41 days off work. The experience, she said, had left her wary of people and unable to continue a normal life.

As expert witness, Dr David Shevel described Sandy's psychiatric condition and said that she'd been treated for suicidal tendencies, while 'Miss Clinton-Parker had gone through a phase of alcohol abuse in an attempt to "medicate" herself and avoid her recurrent thoughts of the incident.'

He was backed up by Jayni Bloch, who agreed that the women's depression resulted from a severe sense of loss, as well as from feelings that they couldn't cope. They'd been single mothers with their first children. They hadn't opted for abortion or adoption. They'd committed themselves and begun bonding with their unborn children. After the births, they'd bonded in such a way to children who hadn't been born to them that they couldn't swap. The children, in turn, loved the only mothers they knew.

In cross-examination, Counsel for the Defence, Johann du Plessis SC, said neither 'Ms Bloch nor Dr Shevel had extensive experience in respect of psychological trauma suffered by single mothers'. He said if a cross-section of mothers had been subjected to the same stressors as Megs and Sandy, the majority wouldn't suffer the same extreme consequences. Jayni Bloch disagreed, saying it would have been out of the ordinary not to suffer consequences and that she'd be surprised if anyone could handle such a situation without assistance.

Psychologist Anne-Marie Wentzel, who testified in support of the state, had extensive experience with single mothers.

Megs and Sandy bristled when Wentzel took the stand. They disliked her intensely from the evaluation sessions they'd had with her. She'd made them feel they were making a fuss about nothing much and that they didn't have the inner strength to deal with their situation.

Wentzel testified that in her two years of work with unmarried mothers who'd undergone traumas, she had not experienced a case where the consequences were as severe as in this one.

Giving evidence in Afrikaans, Wentzel said that it tallied with expectations that a mother would be anxious and depressed, but that she would not expect psychiatric damage of the nature of a 'mixed malady syndrome'.

Justice Navsa would later say of her evidence:

> It is not disputed that the plaintiffs suffer from mixed anxiety depressive disorder, which was caused by the discovery of the swap. Whilst Wentzel has extensive experience in dealing with trauma suffered by single mothers, neither she nor Dr Korb [the other state expert] had any exposure to mothers faced with the 'unique' stressor in this case. ...what is clear is that even on Wentzel's testimony, the number of single young mothers in which a psychiatric illness could be expected is not negligible...

Both parties accepted that the mothers would require psycho-therapy and psychiatric treatment – for a period of four years in the case of Megs and eight years for Sandy – and that they would probably suffer some consequences for the rest of their lives.

But while acknowledging that the women had suffered, the Defence said the court would be setting a South African legal precedent if it awarded damages. It would be the first time that claimants who did not witness the actual incident were awarded psychiatric damages for trauma caused by an unintentional or negligent act.

According to Advocate Du Plessis, such a ruling would 'open the floodgates' for similar claims. Justice Navsa was to say of this contention: 'It is highly unlikely that a decision in favour of the plaintiffs will cause a flood of litigation. This case was dealt with on its merits.'

Du Plessis said that the Judge would have to make a 'quantum leap' in South African law. This was picked up on by newspapers the following day: according to the *Natal Witness* (Thursday, 24 August 1995), 'It would be the first time that so-called "secondary victims" were awarded a claim for trauma caused by an unintentional or negligent act. Du Plessis asked the judge to dismiss both claims with costs.'

It would be another two months before Justice Mahomed Navsa made his ruling. It was one, he told the court, which would require the wisdom of Socrates, Plato and Solomon.

Advocate Con Hartzenberg, who'd never wavered in his belief that the women had been wronged, would later simply describe it as 'a good judgment and one that will stand as long as the legal system'.

The Wisdom of Solomon

Johannesburg, South Africa
Associated Press
October 21 1995

A judge has awarded damages to two women who
raised each other's babies after learning that the infants
were switched at birth in a government hospital. The
Rand Supreme Court ordered the Gauteng Provincial
Government to pay $50 000 to Sandra Dawkins, 32, of
Johannesburg and $43 000 to Meg Clinton-Parker, 33,
of Pietermaritzburg ... 'the dilemma they found themselves in was not of their own doing', wrote Justice
Mahomed Navsa.

In his 72-page judgment, Navsa concluded:

Having regard to South African authorities and consi-
dering the cases in other jurisdictions I can see no reason

in principle or policy why the plaintiffs should not succeed in their claims. In my view, the harm suffered by the plaintiffs is sufficiently close to the defendant's negligence for liability on the defendant's part to arise. I accordingly hold that the defendant is liable to the plaintiffs for the damages sustained by them.

MS NAVSA

JUDGE OF THE SUPREME COURT

That Sunday, 22 October 1995, most South African newspapers carried the story:

BABY SWAP MUMS WIN DAMAGES

CASE MAKES LEGAL HISTORY

BABY SWAP MUMS COMPENSATED
FOR ANGUISH

MA'S KRY R342 072 OOR OMGERUILDE
BABAS*

MONEY CAN'T BRING BACK MY
SWAPPED SON

Money, what money? Sandy and Megs would later ask themselves as they counted the cost of the court action. They both owed Richard Stretch a considerable amount for his services over four years.

* Mothers get R342 072 in swapped babies case

Megs had borrowed money from her father to buy a car. She'd borrowed from her mother's pension for the down-payment towards legal fees. Richard Stretch's father had lent them money and Richard had advanced her R20 000 to buy a bike for Gavin and for an overseas trip. The court award was R158 248 with interest of 15,5% from date of judgment to date of payment and the state was ordered to pay Con's and Sandy Sarantos' costs. 'I ended up with R13 000 cash and the car,' Megs says wryly.

Sandy got R183 824, R25 000 more than Megs because of her circumstances, ruled Navsa.

> As far as Dawkins was concerned it was common cause that because she had less of a family support structure, she was not able to cope with the situation as well as Clinton-Parker. Her condition is well-documented. She has clearly suffered greatly since the discovery of the swap in 1990. She will require psychotherapy lasting several years. The experts agree that the problem will always be with the plaintiffs. Dawkins' work performance had suffered greatly and she has not pursued her studies. I have already described the loss both plaintiffs have suffered as mothers and the investments they have made in the children handed to them by the hospital...

Megs, whose health has never recovered from the shock of the swap and years of subsequent stress, jokingly says her supportive relationship with John Lubbe, now her husband, cost her R25 000. But she agrees that John certainly set her on the right path. 'There is no question that had he not moved in when he did I would be anorexic and in a far worse emotional state. John has kept an eye on my eating and provided a loving, affectionate relationship for both myself and Gavin,' she says.

Of the R183-odd thousand, Sandy eventually received R49 000 cash in 1997, almost two years after judgment. She had been hoping to buy the townhouse she'd been living in, but by 1997 she had to move back to her mom's with Robin and Jessica.

★

In France in 2015, two families whose daughters were switched at birth in 1994 won two million euros in compensation. A court ordered that the Cannes clinic at the centre of the mix-up pay 400 000 euros to each of the swapped babies, by then adult women, 300 000 to three parents and 60 000 euros to three siblings.

At the time, says Stretch, their amounts had seemed fair: 'If it were the US, it would have been a massive claim. But we had to be wary. We knew the state would argue that Megs and Sandy should have given the children back, then they wouldn't have incurred all these costs – like the travelling.'

A Law Letter in July 1996 comments:

> Generally, South African courts are wary about granting damages for emotional shock, because to do so in one set of circumstances might well open a floodgate of other similar claims. But in this case, the facts were unique and the mothers had undoubtedly suffered severe emotional distress as a result of the negligence of the hospital authorities.

Sandy is bitter about the amount they received.

'It's a sore point. If it had depended on me, I would have sued the state for a minimum of R2-million. But everyone was nervous. I didn't like anything about the way the finances were handled. I had asked Richard for a monthly account, but he told me it would be added to the amount we were going to sue for. It wasn't. The bill of costs was supposed to be handed in for taxation to the state attorney before the case started, but it was only handed in afterwards and I was then told that the money was only payable upon completion of the taxation.'

Advocate Con Hartzenberg says attorney and own client fees and expenses are always far in excess of what's recovered from the other party.

'You have a system of taxation of legal fees and expenses and after judgment it's the attorney's job to sit with the taxing master and the registrar of the High Court and the other side and their cost consultants. There are set tariffs for things like writing a letter, or answering a phone call, preparing photo-copies, preparing six sets of documents. The opposite party will dispute the most trivial of things to bring the cost down. And those tariffs bear no relation to the actual fees and expenses charged.'

Megs says they didn't go to court for the money – it was to set a precedent. But she was unhappy with the quantum aspect. The amount allocated for transport – R1 per kilometre – was ridiculous and she feels it contributed to her not having regular and proper access to Robin.

'In divorce cases, the spouse who does not have custody has access at least every second weekend,' she says. 'We should have been allowed the same. Furthermore, the calculations were based on road travel and I believe they should have been based on air travel, so that visitation could have been maximised. Nor was it factored in that we would need accommodation when we travelled to Johannesburg to see Robin.'

That's simply the way it is, says Hartzenberg. 'There is usually a 40 per cent shortfall between what you spend and what you are able to account for. Counsel stayed in the equivalent of a Holiday Inn when we came up to Johannesburg, but the tariffs didn't even cover that. Travel expenses at the time for us were akin to a second-class train ticket.'

So Megs and Sandy were left to pay the shortfall. The invoices kept coming.

> Dear Megs
> I regret to advise that when attending to the final accounting, the airfare in respect of Con Hartzenberg's trip to Johannesburg when he attended the taxation was unfortunately omitted. I hereby enclose a statement in respect of your half share. R465.50

Megs has tried to rationalise all of this, saying that whatever they got out, the case was important because it had enabled them to blame the establishment. Sandy, she still feels, blames her: for having had the baby in Nigel, for insisting on blood tests, for refusing to give up Gavin or let her adopt Robin; for eventually taking Robin away from her.

★

Recriminations aside, they did set a precedent. While this may have been the first case of its kind in South African legal history, it wasn't the last. South Africa was to enter the strange-but-true record books again when it was revealed in 2014 that nurses at the Tambo Memorial Hospital in Benoni, east of Johannesburg, had somehow managed to exchange a boy and a girl. It's the first known case where children of a different gender have been swapped.

One of the mothers, N, a diabetic, had had a Caesarean on 2 August 2010, but was awake throughout. She was shown her baby girl immediately after birth, before a nurse took the child away. Interviewed by *Carte Blanche* on M-Net in 2014, she said she'd passed out soon afterwards.

'I regained consciousness after a few days,' she recalled. 'When I saw the other mothers with their kids, I wanted my baby with me. So I asked the sister in charge if I could see my child. She said he was in the children's ward. I said: "*him*"?'

There was only one child in the ward and he had a tag with 'N' written on it attached to his wrist. She told the sister there must have been a mistake because she'd been shown a baby girl after the birth. The sister laughed and said she must have been confused because she was ill. When she insisted that the child had been a girl, she was accused of trying to reject her baby. She remained doubtful, but was eventually persuaded that she'd been mistaken.

'I sat there looking at him and suddenly I fell in love with this child and I couldn't stop loving him. And I begged God to forgive me for being doubtful,' she told the interviewer

She and her baby boy were discharged and that, she said, was that, until three years later when his father refused to pay maintenance. They had an older son together as well and he looked nothing like his brother. Like Megs, N approached the courts and DNA tests were ordered.

'I went with all the confidence because I never cheated on him and I knew exactly he was the father. But I got the shock of my life … The DNA tests came back and they told me I wasn't the mother and he wasn't the father … I went straight back to the hospital where I gave birth and told them their mistake. At first they thought we were kidding, but we had proof. I had results saying I was actually raising a child that was not mine.'

There had been 11 children born by C-section on the day the boy was born, in five different operating theatres, on different floors. From the records, hospital authorities narrowed down possible swaps to eight children, then to three, then two males and a female child. They saw a pattern: the same midwife had attended to both mothers, although the Caesareans were done in different theatres. And they took into account that N had told them her baby was a girl, but she had been given a boy.

By this process of elimination, hospital authorities worked out that the boy had been swapped with a baby girl. Her 'mother' H had been put onto oxygen straight after the birth and the baby taken to a separate ward.

It appeared that the files and/or name tags had been accidentally swapped by the midwife. Every mother's admission file at the hospital has two blank tags inside, one for the baby, one for the mother. So the tags were filled in before the birth and before the genders had been determined instead of in theatre, after the birth. The tags were then either put in the wrong file, or the wrong files were taken to each theatre. So the file accompanying H contained a tag for N's baby and vice-versa.

H was contacted and told to urgently come to the Tambo Memorial Hospital, because the Department of Health needed to tell her something about her baby. They sat her down and told her she needed to have blood tests because of a suspected mix-up. Disbelieving, she had the tests at a lab in Johannesburg, saying she'd kill herself if her little girl wasn't hers. She was so shocked when the results confirmed that she wasn't her little girl's mother that she had to be admitted to the Charlotte Maxeke Hospital in a state of emotional collapse. There she was put in the care of professional therapists.

Both mothers were interviewed by Advocate Ann Skelton of the Centre for Child Law. Coincidentally, 23 years earlier, Richard had written to Ann and she had helped facilitate funding for Megs' and Sandy's litigation. In this case, she was asked by the North Gauteng High Court to compile a report on whether swapping the children back would be in their best interests.

She interviewed the fathers: the man who'd believed he was the baby girl's father, although in a relationship with H, was married to someone else, but had no other children. It had taken a series of delicate family negotiations to get the child accepted. She was given the same name as his mother and traditional ceremonies were performed. He compared the shock of finding out that he wasn't her father to losing a limb.

The other father, who had initially not wanted anything to do with the mix-up, now didn't want to lose the son who wasn't his, because the little boy was close to his older son. But he expressed a desire to get to know his biological daughter.

His former partner N was adamant she wanted her biological child back. She told *Carte Blanche*: 'I want my child back and I still do. I think of all the experiences I could've gone through with her while I was busy raising someone else's child, regardless of the memories that I have with him and some are very wonderful memories. I just feel like I really need my own child back.'

A team of therapists began working with the mothers and children, bringing them together in contact sessions and providing individual therapy. N described the moment she saw her little girl: 'Oh my God, I was so happy just seeing her for the first time … she was shy, she didn't talk much. She just kept quiet, we played tea, she made me tea and we drank it. The only sad part was that I saw her for that short time and wasn't going home with her. My heart broke when we had to separate.'

Asked by presenter Bongani Bingwa if she would like to swap the babies, she replied: 'As much as I would love to keep my son, I really can't. I have to be with my little girl. I have to see for myself the changes she will go through and all the stuff she has to face. I need her to be with me. On the outside I may look strong and am able to face the world, inside I am just torn apart, I am a wreck. It hurts. I think about if she is being taken care of, does she take a bath before going to bed? As much as I don't want to swap, I need my own flesh and blood next to me.'

Skelton would explain to her that a court would have to make that decision based on the best interests of the child and not merely on the issue of biology.

Group sessions with the children showed that each mother had bonded and that placing the children back with their biological mothers was unlikely to succeed, particularly as the children were now four years old. Psychological assessments showed that the little boy was anxiously attached to N and constantly sought reassurance from her. Her biological daughter was securely attached to H, who was devastated by any talk of losing her. 'If the court tells me to swap I will kill myself,' she promised.

Skelton recommended that the children stay with the parents who'd raised them and should also be permitted to have contact with their biological parents.

When they heard about the latest swap Megs and Sandy got in touch, even though they hadn't spoken in years.

'I got on the blower pretty much straight away,' says Megs. 'I thought: I need to speak to her. She answered when I phoned. It was like yesterday all over again.'

Sandy says she sobbed her heart out.

'I thought, these poor women, do they know what they will go through? And when I heard the one mother say the nurse had told her she must be confused, I got furious all over again. Had no lessons been learnt? Surely there was a foolproof system of tagging babies? Why don't they do it before the umbilical cord is cut?'

At least, says Sandy, the Health Department had, in this latest case, had the decency to call H to a meeting, rather than just blurt it all out over the phone as the Nigel Hospital had done with her 25 years ago, and then offered her no discernable support.

The Impossible Choice

Lawyer Richard Stretch was interviewed in 1996 by Richard Carleton of *60 Minutes*:

Richard Carleton (RC): 'What is the legal position now?'

Richard Stretch (RS): 'It's uncertain. At any time any one of them could change her mind and demand her biological child back.'

RC: 'And the law would support her?'

RS: 'Yes.'

RC: 'What happens if one mother snatches her biological child back?'

RS: 'I don't think it would be defined as a snatch. She would be taking her own child back.'

RC: 'That's an impossible situation!'

RS: 'They will suffer for the rest of their lives, know-ing someone else is caring for their child, not knowing how the child is being cared for, whether it's being properly clothed or fed, whether it is happy or sad. They will miss all those things that a parent is entitled to enjoy. That's why we have children: to watch them grow up. Neither of them will watch their children grow up. That's their agony.'

★

Christmas 1990 had evoked few feelings of peace or goodwill in Sandy. Her resentment against Megs, the hospital nurses and whatever gods had conspired against her only grew. She'd been looking forward to the festive season with her family and little Robin, now old enough to recognise Santa and unwrap presents. Instead, uppermost in all their minds was that he wasn't actually theirs. Their son, nephew and grandson lived in Pietermaritzburg.

Sandy had spent 22 months watching the baby boy she'd brought home from hospital achieving his milestones.

'I'd been looking forward to bringing my boy to maturity the old-fashioned way. By working hard to support him and spending time with him after work and weekends; going to the park, teaching him to play cricket, how to ride his bike, watching his excitement when he got reimbursed for his first tooth … suddenly I felt cheated.'

She'd nursed him through colic, measles and bronchial pneu-monia, watched him sit by himself at five months and take his first tentative steps eight months later.

'He was exactly 13 months when he got up and started walking around after the dog. It was so sweet to see...'

Her moods fluctuated wildly. Sometimes she wondered if she should take back her biological child, whom she hardly knew, before it was too late. But most of the time she wished the Clinton-Parkers would disappear out of their lives and leave her and Robin alone.

'I had been handed a baby I hadn't brought into the world. But funnily enough, it made me try even harder to be the perfect mom. Maybe, I thought, it was all a mistake and I would prove that by trying harder. How could he not be mine?'

The only way he could become hers was if she legally adopted him. For that she needed Megs' consent.

★

In Pietermaritzburg, Megs somehow got through Christmas. As soon as the festive season was over, she began consulting experts about the way forward. Adopting their current children was one option. Swapping them back was the other.

In 1988, when Joan had first found out that Megs was pregnant, she'd insisted she consult Child Welfare to consider having her child adopted straight after birth. She was a single working mother and this might be best, Joan thought.

Megs didn't want to do anything of the sort, but went along with her mother's wishes and spoke to a social worker called Miss Terry, who told her adopted children were always placed in a similar or better environment to the one in which they were born. Megs listened, but remained adamant she wasn't going to give up her baby.

Now, they turned to Child Welfare again, the circumstances this time very different and far more complex. The organisation had a panel of experts it consulted when the need arose, among them legal minds and psychologists. But they'd never dealt with a baby swap.

> The psychologist acknowledges that this is the first case of this nature in which he has been asked to become involved. A literature study and consultation has failed to identify any study with direct bearing on the matter at hand.
> Clive Willows
> Clinical Psychologist

Willows had looked at the effects of divorce on children and the effects on parents after the loss of a child; the adjustment of adopted and fostered children; the psychological effects of bonding – and at examples of Jewish parents returning to reclaim their children left in the care of Dutch foster parents after the Second World War.

Based on this, some members of the panel advised swapping the boys back before they were two-and-a-half. They were about to turn two. But it could be a very different scenario in 10 years' time, said Willows.

> The children's response to their situation if they are not swapped is unpredictable. Adolescence is a time

of identity formation, based in part with a teenager coming to terms with his roots and the history of his family. The process will be directly affected by the fact that they are not growing up in their 'own' family. There may be a need to identify more strongly with their biological families.

Megs and Joan felt they were being given textbook answers to a situation that wasn't textbook. They felt they were being pre-scribed to instead of consulted and that some of the advice was just plain wrong:

The damage can in either case be equated in part to the emotional damage resulting from the death of a child.

Joan wrote underneath this paragraph: 'No! In death, the child would be removed from the world, but whichever child Megs has to give up would still be alive and a constant source of anxiety about his welfare.'

Joan and Megs requested that the panel meet with all of them, including Richard Stretch and their family physician, Dr Watson, so they could become familiar with both her and Sandy's per-sonal circumstances. But they were informed that this 'was not done'. Nor was baby swapping, Megs retorted.

Eventually, on 7 March 1991, a meeting was arranged at the University of Natal. Megs and Joan were accompanied by Dr Watson, but not Richard Stretch, who'd got lost and couldn't find the venue. They put their concerns to the panel, which included family law professor Michael Lupton.

Megs wonders if she was looking for reasons not to swap back, but she explained to them why she thought that their advice was ill conceived. She told them that when Gavin was 22 months old, he'd had tick bite fever and she'd taken him to the doctor. Months later, he'd say 'doctor!' whenever they drove past the surgery. Now they were trying to tell her he wouldn't be profoundly affected at being taken away from his mother, grandparents, aunts, uncles and cousins?

Not at all, said the panel. Ultimately the decision rested with Megs and Sandy. But if they were going to swap, it had to be done now. Delaying would only make matters worse.

> Due to Gavin's present security and identity with this family, a swap would result in severe emotional trauma. The break in the relationship would not be fully comprehended and may result in retardation in development, anger, depression and guilt. These are typical responses of children of divorced parents.

Clive Willows outlined the implications of Megs' personality type in dealing with her stress.

> Megs prefers an ordered, planned and conventional lifestyle without complicated emotional demands and unexpected changes. Any decision regarding the boys will likely provoke intense feelings of guilt, regret and anger. Either maintaining the status quo or swapping the children would lead to severe trauma of loss. At present she is unable to let go of either child, hence her

wish to care for both ... she is the biological parent
of one child, the psychological parent of the other...

★

Megs and Joan went away from the meeting unresolved. They
began doing their own research, collecting similar cases to theirs.
Joan translated in longhand one that went to court in 1975 –
Petersen and Other vs Kruger and Other. But the parents didn't
sue the state; instead one set sued the other.

On 24 May 1973, a Mrs Petersen was admitted to Tygerberg
Hospital in Cape Town. Her boy, Monray, was born at 11 that
night. At the same hospital, Mrs Kruger had given birth to a son,
David, at 9 pm. The next day, Mrs Petersen was given a child
with 'Kruger' tagged to his ankle. When she pointed this out, the
sister-in-charge took the child and returned with two babies. She
asked Mrs Petersen which one was hers. Mrs Petersen wasn't sure,
but chose the one she thought it was. The child was then brought
back to her with 'Petersen' tagged to his leg. When she got home,
her husband said little Monray looked nothing like their other
children had as babies. Unsure of what to do, they decided to wait
until his features had become more pronounced. So for a year
they parented a child they doubted was theirs. As time passed, it
became evident that little Monray resembled neither his parents
nor his siblings. Everyone commented on it.

In September 1974, Mr Petersen succeeded in finding an
address for the Krugers. He staked out their house until he caught
a glimpse of the child, David, who looked very much like his two
sons back home. The Petersens went to Tygerberg Hospital to

ask for advice. The superintendent referred them to the provincial blood laboratory, which arranged tests for the Petersens, the Krugers and the boys. The tests confirmed that David Kruger belonged to the Petersens; Monray Petersen to the Krugers.

The Petersens were desperate to swap back; the Krugers, who were very attached to David, didn't want to hear about it.

By law, the Petersens were entitled to their biological child. But the authority of the court could intervene if it felt the child's welfare would be threatened. The Petersens applied for an order obliging the Krugers to return David to them. He was now two years old.

The court, having assessed the Petersens' circumstances, granted the order, saying it would not be detrimental to David's physical, moral or psychological welfare if he were returned to his natural parents. Acting Judge President of the Cape, Louis de Villiers van Winsen, said that in certain circumstances parental authority could be interfered with. The judgment ruled that 'The circumstances under which a Court may feel itself called to intervene in parents' right of control and oversight are when the exercise of the aforementioned right may endanger the life, health or moral welfare of the child … but they are not limited to these three: any grounds having bearing on the welfare of the child can serve as reason for the Court's involvement.'

And so, aged two, David left the Kruger household and became Monray Petersen. The boy the Petersens had been bringing up went to live with his biological parents and became David Kruger.

Today, Monray and David are middle-aged men and cannot remember anything about the swap. They attended school in the same area of Cape Town and occasionally played rugby against each other. They even worked together at the Post Office after school.

Monray, now employed at the City of Cape Town, became aware of the swap when he was growing up because the story featured in a magazine, *Keur*, and on *Carte Blanche*. 'Ruda Landman came and spent the day with us,' he remembered. 'I used to wonder how my life would have been if my parents hadn't swapped back. I'm so grateful they did.'

At the heart of Megs' and Joan's reluctance to swap Robin and Gavin was that Sandy's circumstances simply weren't good enough. Joan notes the Petersens' financial stability: 'The Petersens live in a good neighbourhood and because of Mr P's earnings, Mrs P stays at home to look after the children. The moral and religious level of the family is also good. They are no threat to David's well being.'

Megs also felt that neither Sandy nor Jeff understood the long-term implications of the swap and that this placed a burden on her to ensure that circumstances be examined from every angle so that the decision they eventually arrived at was the wisest one.

To Sandy it sometimes all seemed useless and endless: 'See the family lawyer, advocate, consult with psychiatrists, psychologists, go for more blood tests, evaluations. Adopt or swap? The impossible choice …'

★

Sandy had, with some nudging from Joan and Megs, consulted Child Welfare on one of her visits to Pietermaritzburg. It was agreed that she would pay a follow-up visit to Johannesburg Child Welfare and provide them with a full background and medical history, as Megs had done in Pietermaritzburg.

Megs' Child Welfare report was revealing:

> Primary school was completed without significant difficulty. It did become apparent however that Megs suffered from lymphedema, which results in swollen feet ... Megs was not adventurous and apart from the pregnancy had not had to deal with major trauma or confusion. She had the ability to adapt to new circumstances. Megs believes she has changed significantly over the past few years. She has become almost obsessed with her present dilemma and has excluded herself from social contacts. As a way of compensation for her problems she has turned to food and now experiences a weight problem.

The following month, Megs travelled to Johannesburg and she and Sandy had a joint session with Child Welfare there. They both ended up in tears when social workers told them the courts could force them to make a decision, or refer them to a family court to formalise adoption. Today Megs wonders if perhaps her fears were unfounded and the family court could actually have assisted in a proper visitation process and prevented some of the trauma that was to come in her fight for access to Robin.

She asked Child Welfare to share with her details of Sandy's background, so she could assess whether or not she was fit to adopt Robin. She told them the advice she'd received from Pietermaritzburg Child Welfare: that a child should never be placed in a worse environment. They refused to give her any information about Sandy's home life or state of mind.

Sandy resented the intrusion into her life.

'We were not a family who spent weekends visiting all and sundry,' she says. 'We were close knit and private and did not interfere with anyone outside of our home and weren't used to other people interfering in our lives. We were uncomplicated humble people. And I really wanted my personal and family life to stay just that – personal.'

Megs and Joan drew up a list about Sandy: she was 'illegitimate and her parents didn't marry until she was ten'. They found Sandy's 'non-academic' status a problem. She'd left school before finishing, worked as a bank clerk and had done nothing to improve her qualifications or earning power. Nor, according to Megs, did Sandy have a high regard for the truth, often saying one thing and doing another.

Jeff, she noted, although stable in himself, wasn't stable in relationships, with two children from his first marriage and three illegitimate children, two of them with Sandy.

Sandy accused Megs of snobbery and found her objections to having children without being married laughable, the proverbial pot calling the kettle black. Megs says the point is she only made the mistake once.

Megs couldn't stop agonising over her choices:

'If we swap the children my son, Gavin, goes to an environment I have grave reservations about and I have no say about what happens to him, have no influence over him and he will lose the values he has been benefiting from. On the other hand, if my son Robin remains where he is and I do not allow Sandy to adopt him, I can have an influence over him and have a say in important decisions. I can provide books, finance for his education, if I am able. I can have input into the kind of opportunities he gets. I can prevent the occurrence of anything seriously detrimental to him. I am NOT prepared to give up my natural son.'

Despite having seemingly made up her mind, Megs could not let the problem go. She and Joan drew up a list of pros and cons:

SWAP ADVANTAGES:
- Mothers have legal rights to their natural children, no legal problems now or later. Striking likeness to natural families – children would be where they belonged.
- Children would not resent their mother's abandonment.
- No feelings of 'not my child' when discipline issues arise.
- Swapping would be easier to explain to child.
- If swapped before August 1991, children would have no recall of the first two years and would forget the trauma.

SWAP DISADVANTAGES:
- Children have close bond with current families.
- Mothers would find it difficult to accept the swap.
- Could lead to an inconsistent relationship with the child, who may become anxious and insecure.
- Success of this approach would depend on the mothers' responses and attitudes.

ADOPTION ADVANTAGES:
- No short-term trauma for boys and mothers.
- Close bonds between these single mothers and their boys would be maintained.
- Both are good mothers.

- If not adopted, children would be left in legal limbo. Parents could change minds later when much more traumatic for child.

ADOPTION DISADVANTAGES:
- If adopted mother dies, who will have rights over the child?
- As child gets older, could resent being abandoned by natural mother.
- Strong likeness to natural parents could lead to feelings of alienation.
- Not swapping harder to explain to biological child.
- No guarantee of regular contact with natural child.

None of this helped them come to a decision. With Richard Stretch, they drew up a parenting plan, outlining the way forward. If they weren't going to adopt or swap the boys, they needed to set boundaries, to avoid future conflict.

Megs wanted Robin to carry her name as a way of getting some ownership over him. She doubts she would ever have gone through with changing Gavin's surname to Dawkins, but included it in the makeshift parenting plan so it didn't seem unfair. Each mother would have limited power-of-attorney in respect of the child in her custody – such as permission to sign in medical emergencies, although the natural mother had to be informed.

Each mother, could, when possible – as she would in the case of a divorce – have her natural son stay with her for a weekend once a month and the boys should spend holidays together and grow up as brothers. A claim by the natural mother of either child for the return of her natural child from the care of the other would not be made without written notice and each would be entitled to legal representation. Should such an exchange be envisaged, it would be a gradual process and would involve the two mothers living together in surroundings not previously known to either child for a period of up to three months, so that the identification of each boy with his own mother could be effected and trauma minimised.

Each child would receive pre-primary, primary and high school education including matric, followed by tertiary education, agreed upon by the mothers, according to the child's aptitude. Each mother was to have an education policy for the child in her care.

The agreement was presented to Sandy, via Lee Hirschowitz, a lawyer whose services Lister & Lister had employed in Johannesburg.

6 June 1991

Sandy attended at our offices today. She arrived one hour early, accompanied by the child, Robin. She was anxious to clarify her position and asked that I set out her legal options. I explained that her options were three-fold:

To give up the child in her care and take custody of her natural child

To adopt the child in her care and consent to the adoption of her natural child by Megs

To leave matters as they are – that is to continue bringing up Robin as her own child, but to clarify and to enter into an agreement with Megs.

Sandy immediately advised that her first choice would be to adopt Robin and to consent to the adoption of Gavin by Megs. She stated that she was aware that Megs would not consent to such an adoption, so the best possible solution would be to leave things as they were, but to enter into an agreement with Megs. During the course of the consultation, Sandy stated that her greatest fear was that Megs would demand the return of Robin.

Sandy undertook to discuss the agreement with Jeffrey and to revert to me in due course. Her attitude during the course of the consultation was conciliatory and she constantly expressed her wish to resolve these matters on an amicable basis.

She advised that she would be moving in with Jeff during the course of next week. Jeff is the father of her unborn child. She expressed a wish that eventually they will be married but stated that in the meantime she wanted to provide Robin and the child she is expecting, with a stable structure based on a nuclear family unit.

But things between Sandy and Jeff didn't work out. According to Jeff, there wasn't one specific reason – he just wanted more out of life than Sandy.

And so the boys' status remained in limbo. Whatever their differences, Megs and Sandy had inadvertently been drawn into a symbiotic relationship – an enforced dependence that affected them on all levels and wasn't going to go away.

The Media Spotlight

It's a common literary device that's been used in American fiction since the 19th Century by authors like Mark Twain in *The Tragedy of Pudd'nhead Wilson;* by Gilbert and Sullivan in the operas *HMS Pinafore* and *The Gondoliers,* and more recently in *Desperate Housewives.*

The South African TV series, *Uzalo,* explores the lives of two young men who were switched at birth, one of them the child of a priest, the other of a gangster. The drama examines the impact of this discovery on the lives of the criminally minded Xulus and the God-fearing Mdletshes.

A film by French filmmaker Lorraine Levy called *The Other Son* explores the complex repercussions facing two boys, one Palestinian, one Israeli, who were switched. The discovery is made as the Israeli boy is preparing to join the army for national service. His parents are horrified and aren't sure what disturbs them more: that their biological child, Yacine, has been raised on the West Bank as the enemy, or raised in Islam, instead of Judaism.

In another French film, *La Vie est un Long Fleuve Tranquille,* the switch of two babies is discovered when the children are 12.

Again one family is affluent, with dutiful and apparently con-
tented children, the other is poor with delinquent children in a
happy household.

One of the highest rated TV series in the States is called, surprise-
surprise, *Switched at Birth* and revolves around two teenage girls
who have grown up in very different environments, one in an
old money suburb in Kansas, the other in a working-class part of
Missouri. One of the teens discovers – in her school science lab
of all places – that her blood type isn't compatible with that of
her parents, and the familiar tale of a well-born baby switched
with a commoner emerges. The well-to-do family invites their
biological daughter and her single mother to live with them.
Happily-ever-after? Not always.

It's a great plot and one that never tires. So when it happens in
real life, there's no holding back the public interest.

One of the most famous real-life switch stories is that of Mary
Miller and Kay McDonald, two women from Wisconsin whose
babies were accidentally switched in hospital in 1951. What made
this case remarkable was that the two women knew each other
and that Miller suspected the switch had taken place, but didn't
do anything because her husband told her she was being silly and
that she would embarrass the family doctor. So she stifled her
motherly instinct for 43 years until her husband died, because she
'didn't want to make waves'. The story was told on *This American
Life*, a weekly public radio show.

The switch of Robin Dawkins and Gavin Clinton-Parker was
the first case in South Africa to make legal history by suing the
state for damages. Once it was known, Megs and Sandy found
themselves thrust into the media spotlight. A reporter from the

Natal Witness first found out about the impending case, but was put off by Richard Stretch, who said he could neither confirm nor deny there'd been a swap. Apart from wanting to protect the boys, Megs hadn't yet told her extended family about the swap. They still thought Gavin was hers.

According to Megs, they'd been advised by their attorney not to act independently and not to breathe a word to the press. Sandy's understanding, it seemed, was different.

'I didn't really give a hoot,' she says. 'I wasn't keeping it a secret. Although I didn't tip off the *Witness*, contrary to what people might've thought.'

In late May 1991, Richard had a phone call from *Rapport* newspaper. They wanted to speak to Megs. Sandy had granted them an interview. Not only Sandy – she seemed to have given *Rapport* access to her entire family, without telling Megs, or the lawyers.

Megs and Richard felt Sandy was jeopardising the case by speaking out without first consulting them. Sandy pleaded innocence: 'The reporter arrived at my house one night out of nowhere after they had gotten my details from the Nigel Hospital and my house doctor.'

They pitched up at Jeff's workplace too, presumably having also got the address from the hospital.

The story would be published that coming Sunday. Megs simply couldn't cope with the whole world knowing. Not yet. The court case would be bad enough.

Richard applied for an urgent interdict to stop the publication of the article.

24 May 1991

Dear Megs

INTERDICT RAPPORT

Herewith our entire file. Ms Lee Hirshowitz will be acting on your behalf for the interdict. She is situated at Suite 1232, Kine Centre, 141 Commissioner Street, Johannesburg. It is necessary for you to consult with her and Advocate Kuper first thing tomorrow morning. You and Sandra should arrange a time for this purpose.

I am sorry I will not be there. Good Luck!

Richard Stretch
Lister & Lister

Megs' father Peter paid the legal costs and she and her sister Pat drove up to Jo'burg. They met with Sandy and the legal team to find out what exactly she'd said and how much of their lives was going to be splashed over *Rapport* the following morning. After an urgent interdict, they succeeded in getting their names omitted from the article.

On 26 May 1991, *Rapport* ran a watered-down version. Names had been changed, it said, to prevent the boys being stigmatised. Sandy became Linda Bekker and was the mother of Karel, while Megs was the other mother – '*die ander ma*'.

Jeff was called 'Harry'. '*Ek weet nou ek is nie Karel se pa nie,*' he's quoted as saying, *'maar dit maak nie saak wat gebeur nie, hy sal nooit 'n tekort hê aan enigiets nie. Ek sal vir hom sorg so lank as wat ek lewe. Hy glo ek is sy pappie; hy noem my selfs as "daddy"...'*[*]

Jeff recalls being cornered into giving the interview. And that he tried to phone *Rapport* editor, Izak de Villiers, to ask him not to publish the article.

'I hated all the publicity,' he says, 'but they came round to my work and I just tried to get rid of them as quickly as possible.'

In the article, grandmother Kay, renamed Estelle Marx, told of the stress Sandy was undergoing: *'My kind gaan deur diep waters ... as dit tog net kan ophou...'*[**]

The article ends with a quote from Sandy saying that she'd made it clear to Megs that she wanted to adopt Robin – *'as my eie kind, ek het hom so lief'*.[***]

Megs said at the time that this event proved both Sandy's gullibility and downright stupidity – both qualities she saw as detrimental to a child in her care.

Rapport got the message. In July 1993, there was a more inclusive illustrated exclusive:

> *'Eerste fotos van die seuntjies en hulle ma's ... die kleuters is vier en 'n half jaar gelede omgeruil. Vandag is hulle soos broertjies en sien mekaar gereeld ...'*[****]

---

[*] I do know I'm not Karel's father, but it doesn't matter what happens, he'll never want for anything. I'll look after him as long as I live. He believes I'm his dad; he even calls me daddy...

[**] My child is facing tough times ... if it would only just stop...

[***] I love him like he was my own.

[****] First photos of the boys and their mothers ... the toddlers were swapped four and a half years ago. Today they're like brothers and see each other often ...

The article was accompanied by a picture of Gavin and Robin staring at the camera, their arms round each other's necks, and another lying on the grass, looking carefree.

Media interest built up to a peak during the court case. On 28 August 1994 the headlines blared in anticipation of the judgment:

> *HOF sê môre oor omruilbabas*
> *Môre is D-dag vir twee ma's wie se baba-seuntjies byna ses jaar gelede omgeruil is … Oplaas het die ma's verlede jaar besluit om nie langer te talm nie. Die volle waarheid moes uit. Op 11 Julie 1993 het landwyd opskudding verwerk toe die waarheid eksklusief met fotos in Rapport onthul is.* *

During the court case, when Megs was staying in Johannesburg, *Rapport* flew her back to Pietermaritzburg one afternoon to pick up Gavin for a family photo-shoot. She got off the plane, fetched him from her waiting sister and flew back. They were photographed outside the Nigel hospital, already a very different place to the whites-only institution it had been in 1989. The name had changed to the Thabong Clinic – 'place of happiness' – and there wasn't a pale face in sight, apart from Megs, Joan and Peter Clinton-Parker, Sandy, her mother Kay and sister Lynette. Joan's hands rest on Robin's shoulders, Megs holds possessively onto Gavin. Sandy squints into the sun, her hands behind her back.

---

* Court to pronounce on swapped babies tomorrow: Tomorrow is D-day for two mothers whose baby sons were swapped almost six years ago … Finally, last year, they decided to wait no longer. The whole truth must come out. On 11 July 1993 the country was in shock when the truth was revealed with photos in a *Rapport* exclusive.

Although Megs wanted public sentiment on their side, the newspaper reports and magazine articles made her self-conscious.

'We had always been a private family and all of this was very new to us,' she says. 'I didn't enjoy being in the limelight, but realised the publicity was good for the case. Everyone has kids and it freaks them out to think that they might not be theirs.'

★

In September 1993, *YOU* magazine ran what was to be the first of many articles: 'Tormented Mothers' Bitter Choice'. It told of the soul-searching, tears and heartache that had led to the decision not to swap the boys back and instead to try to keep contact despite the distances between them.

The *YOU* stories were picked up by the Australian prime time TV current affairs show *60 Minutes*, which began a working relationship with Megs, Sandy, Robin and Gavin that would span more than two decades.

The first documentary, *The Impossible Choice*, was presented by veteran Aussie journalist Richard Carleton, no stranger to South Africa. His favourite anecdote was how he'd been detained for five hours at the SABC's Auckland Park headquarters, after being accused of breaking censorship laws on the eve of the 1987 election.

Carleton – who once famously provoked former Australian Prime Minister Bob Hawke into losing his temper during an interview – made a habit of becoming the news, even allowing *60 Minutes* cameras to film him having heart bypass surgery. In 2006 he collapsed and died at a press conference in Tasmania, while grilling officials about the Beaconsfield mine tragedy.

The baby swap was a tame one for him. He was used to going for the jugular from strife-torn parts of the world, be it East Timor or the Persian Gulf. Now he was contending with two mothers, who didn't exactly get on, and two boys, one curious, the other terrified that the world as he knew it was about to change.

Carleton and his producer Howard Sacre decided that the 'rich kid poor kid' approach would work well. There was a class difference between Megs and Sandy and the Aussies exploited this to great effect.

According to them, Megs was rich and privileged and Sandy was from the wrong side of the tracks: 'Sandy has no money, no car, she's Afrikaans and walks Robin home to – well – not the best of Johannesburg suburbs. She has no family support. Life for Megs and Gavin has been vastly different. When Gavin goes home it's to his big extended English family in a large comfortable house.'

The camera cuts away to a car wreck; in the background is seven-year-old Robin bringing in the washing. Gavin is seen riding his bicycle and then, dressed in a chef's hat, cooking with Megs in their kitchen in Pietermaritzburg.

In reality, Megs was – and still is – a middle-class South African who drinks run-of-the-mill coffee and can just afford a flat-screen TV and an occasional holiday. She's been working in municipal finance at a dull government building in downtown Pietermaritzburg for close on 25 years.

At first, she and Gavin lived with her parents in their rambling old house in Scottsville. Later, after she'd married John, a fitter and turner, they moved to a comfortable, but certainly not affluent, area.

'I remember a friend reading some of the stuff written about us and saying: 'Hell Megs, when did you get rich?' she laughs.

★

'The Impossible Choice' was to be the first of many stories with *60 Minutes*. Over the years, the Australians dipped in and out of the boys' lives.

> Presenter Liz Hayes in 2000: 'Robin lives on the poor side of town with Sandy. Gavin grew up in a far wealthier area with Megs, whom he calls his mum.'

> Peter Overton in 2004: 'Today they're teenagers, having grown up living the other's life. For one it has been a tough life on the breadline, while the other has struck it lucky.'

Lucky Gavin was at a good state school, and spent weekends camping, fishing at the Albert Falls Dam, biking, or playing golf with stepfather John.

Part of Robin's early years were spent in a flat south of Johannesburg, with Sandy and her daughter Jessica, who was the image of Gavin Clinton-Parker. When Richard Carleton and *60 Minutes* arrived at Sandy's flat in February 1996 to set up for an interview, there was no furniture to sit on. So producer Howard had a cane lounge suite delivered within the hour.

In the story, Sandy sits on her new furniture, explaining for the umpteenth time what she felt when she first learned of the swap: 'My immediate reaction was "I am not going to swap Robin back. He's mine and that's the way it's going to stay..."'

The story is a happy one, full of hope that somehow these two

LEFT Megs and Gavin at eight months
ABOVE Robin at eight months
BELOW First meeting: Sandy, Robin,
Gavin and Megs at the beach

OPPOSITE: TOP Megs, Gavin and his biological father Jeff Parsons – first meeting
MIDDLE LEFT Feeding the pigeons: Gavin and Robin (standing)
BOTTOM LEFT Dave's mother Margaret with her youngest son Hyde, whom
everyone thought resembled Robin
RIGHT Joan Clinton-Parker and Gavin one month after learning that he was
not her grandson
THIS PAGE: TOP On Jeff's motorbike in Nigel: Robin and Sandy
LEFT Robin aged two   RIGHT Robin and Gavin with his biological sister
Jessica, Sandy's daughter, 1991

TOP Making headlines in *Rapport*: Gavin and Robin, aged five
Photo courtesy *Rapport*
LEFT Gavin in Grade 1
RIGHT Gavin in Grade 5 – second row from back, third from left

ABOVE Back to where it happened. Posing for *Rapport* outside Nigel Hospital in August 1995: Sandy, Megs, Gavin and Robin

LEFT Megs marries John Lubbe with Gavin by her side, 1996

TOP Backstage at the Maury Povich Show,
April 1996. From left to right: producer,
Megs, Maury, John, Sandy, Gavin, Jessica
and Robin

ABOVE LEFT Enjoying a New Jersey theme
park after the Maury Povich Show, 1996:
Robin, Gavin and Jessica

ABOVE RIGHT Gavin tries on a 50-gallon
hat at the theme park

RIGHT Sandy, Megs and children on
Staten Island, New York, 1996

TOP LEFT Gavin Clinton-Parker and Robin Dawkins aged 11
TOP RIGHT Robin with his biological father, Dave Lotter, in 2007
ABOVE LEFT AND RIGHT Gavin Clinton-Parker aged 13 and 15
LEFT Robin Dawkins with his biological grandfather, Peter Clinton-Parker, in 2006

TOP *60 Minutes* shoot, 2015. Seated, from left: Robin, Megs, Sandy and Gavin face the crew
LEFT Robin, his wife Liezl and their sons Daniel and James
MIDDLE Sandy, Gavin, Megs and Robin
BOTTOM MIDDLE Robin as an adult
BOTTOM RIGHT Gavin as an adult

women will become sisters, who can share their sons. It ends with the boys celebrating their seventh birthday party together and a last interview: the four of them cuddling together on a bench, the boys with wet hair after swimming.

Megs: 'We've become family.'

Sandy: 'We have to support one another ... we are the only ones that really know ...'

'... what's going on...' interjects little Robin and they all laugh.

Richard Carleton: 'Tell me kids, do you think that you are lucky because in a way you have two mums?'

Gavin: 'Ja!'

Robin: 'We're happy!'

Richard: 'Is it difficult when you come together?'

Sandy: 'Getting together is not the difficult part, it's leaving each other, that's the worst.'

★

Staying happy and amicable proved to be easier said than done, on an all-expenses-paid trip to New York, a few months later in April 1996.

With them were Megs' husband, John, and Sandy's daughter Jessica. They were to be guests of Maury Povich, the US tabloid talk show host, who explores family and relationship issues. The most common topic is paternity testing: mothers attempting to prove, or in some cases disprove, who the biological fathers of their children are.

Megs recalls parts of the trip being a strain, with John and Sandy 'boxing all the way': 'She was always late for everything. We had limited time there and we wanted to explore, but Sandy was forever fiddling around in her room ... with Robin, who wanted to be out and about with us...'

John was irritated by Sandy's wild spending: 'She would buy rubbish ... like portable telephones of all shapes and sizes. What for? She had no idea. Instead of buying a suitcase to put it all in, on the flight home she and Robin and Jessica were laden with packets and bags full of the stuff she'd wasted money on.'

Sandy insists it was John who was the irritant, dragging his golf clubs across the Atlantic, not to mention being arrested at passport control at Johannesburg International because his ex-wife had thought he was skipping the country to avoid paying maintenance for their daughter: 'I remember Gavin rushing to tell me in a state that John had been arrested ... they had to phone Richard Stretch to sort it out, leaving Megs stuck with all their luggage – THREE big suitcases ... we had one case between three of us...'

Megs wrote in her travel journal on 19 April 1996:

> 'At checking in our worst nightmare materialised in the form of the ex of course ... and John got arrested! Phoned Richard immediately and John and I were

forced to separate. By this time I was beyond hysteria. I boarded the plane feeling completely drained and beaten. I hoped until the end that John would make the flight but the plane took off without him...

'The flight was long, long, long ... no knowledge regarding John was awful, but I had to put my faith in Richard once again...

'We were met at the airport by a luxury limousine, which lifted our spirits quite radically. The kids were in their element and Howard the driver was most informative and helpful. We checked into our hotel in Manhattan and received the best news that John will arrive tomorrow at 1.30 New York time.'

It wasn't their only brush with the law. Megs remembers two policemen reprimanding Sandy while they were walking down Lexington Avenue. They told her if she didn't stop shouting at Robin they'd have to take action: 'She was constantly threatening Robin ... "if you don't behave I'll knock your block off" kind of stuff ... it really got to us ... and this cop thought she was serious. He said: "I can hear you're not from here, ma'am, but if you were, I would remove this child from your custody."'

Sandy remembers it as no big deal and that she was merely trying to control her excitable son, who was at risk of being run over in the busiest city they'd ever been in. She'd always thought that Megs' idea of discipline was 'a tap with an elastic band'.

Despite their differences, they also had lots of fun together, says Megs: 'There was a genuine affection between Sandy and me and the boys and a sense of unity in a strange country. We were friends and the boys were friends. Sandy and I had our squabbles, but stood up for each other. We loved the limos and the window shopping and had a blast at the Jekyll and Hyde theme restaurant. When we went to the loo, it flushed with Sandy sitting on it – unheard of in those days. She shot out of there like she was being chased. We screeched with laughter.'

She wrote in her journal:

> *Monday 22 April 1996:* 'Up at 5am to go to the studios. Met Preston Goddard and had make-up and hair done ... if you can call that hair "done". Saw the tap-ing of the first show with Jack Hannah as his guest and were allowed behind stage to play with some of the animals. Then we were up. Sandy ended up with a fluffy Angora rabbit on her lap like a blanket, which tickled the kids. Our bit went well.'

They made the most of the limelight because it enabled them to be with their boys in an environment they would otherwise not have been able to afford.

★

In 1997, they were approached by an American film producer to sell their story and were interviewed at length by producer Arlene Sarner, the screenwriter for *Peggy Sue Got Married*.

They felt fine about accepting money for the movie and the *60 Minutes* interviews because, they reasoned, production com-panies had no problem exploiting their misfortune for profit.

There was an emotional price that went with reliving the births, discovery of the switch and heartache in between.

The eventual film, *Two Babies Switched at Birth,* starred Melissa Gilbert as Megs and Rosanna Arquette as Sandy. It grated Megs because it departed so much from reality. Her character, married to Mr Perfect, was a super-rich bitch; Sandy's a sweet arty type who made pottery and had an unsuitable drifter lover who accused her of sleeping around when he saw his son for the first time. Sandy's character, Linda, is the one desperate to meet her biological offspring when the switch is first discovered while the Megs character, Sarah, buries her head in the sand. Eventually though, she and her husband become far too involved in their biological son's life, wanting to decide on and pay for his schooling and set him and his mother up in a house close by.

The vague similarity here is that Megs once suggested to Sandy, as a possible solution, that she and Robin move to KwaZulu-Natal to be closer to them, although nothing ever came of it.

Like Robin as a baby, one of the little boys in the movie is sickly. After he's admitted to hospital with seizures, there's an amusing scene in which the doctor says only his parents can be at his bedside and four of them push past him.

The court case in the film isn't about damages but about custody, with the drifter father, played by Darryll Moncton, out to make money from the situation. It's something both Robin and Gavin's biological fathers, Dave and Jeff, accuse Sandy and Megs of doing at the expense of their children.

Megs is indignant: 'Dave and Jeff have no idea what they're talking about. I was very selective and turned away loads of interviews I felt would have exposed the boys, regardless of the offer on the table. I avoided Oprah because it was screened in South Africa and accepted offers that enabled us to have a holiday together. The trip to New York was a great experience for the boys, but there was no cash, just an all-expenses-paid trip. We got $100 a day for meals per family.'

Sandy remembers the money from the movie being used up in a flash to catch up on utility bills that had piled up, pay school fees in arrears and to buy groceries to fill empty cupboards.

There was a second trip to the US in September 1998, again to appear on the Maury Povich show. This time they featured with Paula Johnson, the mother of a three-year-old American girl, Callie, who'd been switched at a hospital in Virginia. The couple that had been bringing up Paula's biological child, Rebecca, were killed in a car crash the day after Paula got the results of the DNA test she'd had to determine paternity. Rebecca had been in the care of her grandparents, who were then delivered a double blow: their grandchild wasn't actually theirs. Paula left Rebecca in their care, but in later years struggled to obtain custody and visitation rights. When she challenged it, a court found that the girls were old enough to decide for themselves. In the end, Rebecca had limited contact with Paula, but Callie would occasionally visit her biological relatives.

Megs feels emotional remembering Paula's story. She feels she was the 'Sandy' of the switch – without means and stability.

'Paula was still in shock when we met her. She'd just found out. I don't think she really knew what trauma she would face and we tried to offer her what advice we could. Both Sandy and I felt deep empathy for her. We mistakenly thought we'd been through the worst of it.'

Studies cited on the show found that up to half a million children could be swapped at hospitals in the US every year. Finding out about it was a topic that fascinated.

★

When the boys were 11, *60 Minutes Australia* flew them to Cape Town. Megs and John and Gavin; Sandy, Robin and Jessica checked into family rooms at the Mount Nelson Hotel. This time the producer was Gareth Harvey, a seasoned documentary-maker and Emmy Award winner. 'It's a fascinating story,' he said, 'because everyone is able to imagine it happening to them. And it's one of those stories that gets more interesting with each chapter … that's why we keep coming back.'

Mindful that they're intruding, *60 Minutes* always makes sure the location is attractive, the hotel up-market, so that their case studies are comfortable. But they can't pre-arrange the weather. It was a freezing July weekend in the Mother City. An Antarctic wind had deposited a layer of snow on top of Table Mountain.

In the resultant story, this time called 'Nature versus Nurture' there's a shot in the cable car of Megs with her hands on Robin's shoulders looking at the view, while Gavin and Sandy fool around, posing for photographs.

Presenter Liz Hayes tells the camera that 'One of the most extraordinary things for me is seeing these two children together and how mature they seem to be about the situation.'

Megs tells her the boys grew up feeling threatened and that's what made them close: 'I think they thought if we can just get on, then we can all carry on seeing each other.'

There's a two-shot of Gavin and Robin, both expressing fears of change, Robin more articulately than Gavin: 'Rather keep it like it is now … we are used to living where we are. You could break a lot of people's hearts if you swap … It's very sad. You can't do that.'

Gavin just nods furiously next to him.

> Liz Hayes: 'What began as a terrible mistake has been made good by love … Sandy, do you believe your son is in good hands?'

> Sandy: 'He's in excellent hands.'

> Liz: 'Megs, do you feel your son is in good hands?'

> Megs hesitates: 'He's in loving hands.'

The story concludes with goodbyes outside the Mount Nelson. Gavin gives little Robin a bear hug, Megs cries silently as she climbs into the airport shuttle; Sandy plays last touch with Gavin, the boy who shares her blood, but isn't going home with her.

'Love you, Gav!' Robin shouts after the departing minibus.

The story left one with the impression that things might work out.

The War Years

The moment Megs saw Robin she decided she would, one day, get him back. From 500 kilometres away in Pietermaritzburg, she was determined to influence his life. Sandy might love Robin, but Megs felt she lacked the drive to succeed and the qualities to provide her child with education and stability. Wherever home was, in their rootless lives, it was devoid of books, board games or anything that might aid a child's development.

'My expectations for the future cannot be anything less than having both children,' she wrote in a letter to Richard Stretch. 'While this is probably impossible, it is equally impossible for me to envisage either child as being merely adequately taken care of in Sandy's environment. To me they both deserve better – and anything less is not good enough.'

A long-term plan clear in her head, Megs felt the only way forward was to turn a thoroughly negative situation into a positive one. First she had to tell Gavin about the accident of his birth: 'After the court case, win or lose, Gavin has to be told the truth, the effects of which will be devastating to both of us.

This will be done with the assistance of a psychologist.'

The boys had to grow up with full knowledge of what had happened and accept that they had two mothers and two families.

Her mother Joan, an English teacher, wrote a children's story that she planned to read to Gavin and pass on to Sandy to do the same.

Once upon a time two babies were born in a hospital. Both mummies had been looking forward to seeing, holding and loving the babies who had been growing in their tummies...

First Robert was born and the nurse wrapped him up tightly in a warm blanket and his mommy Marge gave him a big hug before the nurse took him to have his first bath...

Soon Gordon was born in the room next door and when he was wrapped up, his mommy Sindy gave him a big hug and the nurses took him away for HIS first bath...

Now somehow the nurses made a terrible mistake. They put the babies in the wrong cots and they hadn't put their names on the arms when they were born, as they should have done because newborn babies look very like each other. And so Robert went home with Sindy and Gordon went home with Marge.

And both mummies cuddled the babes they had, thinking they were their own. They fed them, changed their nappies, hugged them when they cried and loved them very very much.

Then when Gordon and Robert were nearly two, Marge and Gordon had to have some blood tests and the doctor told Marge that she wasn't Gordon's real mommy and she cried and cried and was very sick because she loved Gordon and was afraid that she would have to give him back to his real mommy. When Sindy heard what had happened, she cried and cried too and was very sick and she was afraid that Robert's real mommy might want him back.

And, of course, both mommies wanted their own sons back, but they also wanted to keep the sons they had thought were their own. Poor mommies, they didn't know what to do.

They talked to a lot of clever people and asked them to help them. But some said 'keep the boys you have now and give up your own sons and others said: 'no give back the boys you have now and take your own sons'.

Now the mommies felt as if they each had two sons and so in the end the decided that they would share the boys because the little boys were used to the mommies they had. So in the end the boys stayed where they were and now the mommies and the boys visit each other, they have their birthday parties together and they see each other often and the mommies have two boys and the boys have two mommies and everyone knows that these are very special little boys...

But before they could read the story to Gavin and gradually get him used to such a scenario, something happened that Megs felt made it essential to tell him immediately. And even more determined to get Robin back.

Sandy had become increasingly evasive, with excuses every time Megs tried to make plans for Robin (and Jessica) to visit Pietermaritzburg. She would say one thing and do another. When Megs phoned to speak to Robin, he was never home: 'Oh, you've just missed him ... he's gone to the shop; he's at a friend; he's with his Gran.'

Megs says this went on for six months – she had never felt so helpless in her life. Phone calls to Sandy's mother, Kay, were met with the same hedging. Eventually Megs phoned Sandy at work one day, as Joan Clinton-Parker noted:

'Megs phoned Sandy who was absent without leave. Supervisor let slip she was pregnant (with 3rd illegitimate child – father one presumes is the man who was at court with her last August). He said he and bank staff sorry for Megs as she doesn't know what Sandy is like. Switchboard operators always making derogatory comments about her long phone calls ... he said there was no possibility that she would be transferred to Bloemfontein.'

Megs pretended that she knew what he was talking about. If Sandy was pregnant why hadn't she told them and why had she asked for a transfer to Bloemfontein? Then out of the blue, Joan had a call from Sandy's aunt Gwen, who lived in Bloemfontein with her husband and stepchildren. She said Robin and Jessica had been dumped with her and she hadn't seen Sandy in weeks.

Sandy was in the throes of a nervous breakdown.

'I just gave up,' she says. 'I didn't want to get out of bed in the morning, didn't want to dress, brush my hair ...'

Relieved to have found Robin at last, Joan and Megs kept

contact with Auntie Gwen in Bloem. One day Sandy answered the phone. Yes, she, Robin and Jessica were living there waiting for her transfer, which would be 'any day now'. Yes, they should definitely get together soon. For Christmas or the boys' birthdays? Perfect. There was no mention of the pregnancy.

Whatever the reason for the move, Megs was hugely relieved: at last she had a point of contact. And there were plans to see Robin. Now she could concentrate on her upcoming exams. She was in her first year of a BCom degree through Unisa and she wasn't finding it easy, obsessing about her biological son.

In the meantime, a journalist from *YOU* magazine had phoned Joan, wanting to speak to Megs for an article about to be published. She offered R2000. Megs was on study leave, so Joan referred the request to Richard Stretch. He reported back to Megs that *YOU* needed her comments about an interview Sandy had done.

Megs didn't have the time or the inclination to do it. She and Richard reckoned it would be a rehash anyway, as nothing much had happened in their lives since their last *YOU* spread a year earlier. They were still waiting for the court case and she wasn't going to pour out her heart about Sandy not giving her access to Robin. She dismissed it as just another attempt by Sandy to make some cash.

Until her sister Pat arrived on her doorstep with the *YOU* article. Megs was aghast when she read it. It was headed: 'I Want My Own Child Back ...'

In the interview, done in Bloemfontein, Sandy bemoaned what her life had become: the relationship with the father of her children was in shreds, her colleagues at work were sick and tired of her outbursts, she no longer had any friends and all the unpaid sick leave she'd taken had harmed her financially. And she was being denied access to Gavin:

> 'I'm almost like someone whose child has been kid-
> napped ... the only difference is I know where my
> child is. I won't rest until he's living with me.'

Megs had had no idea Sandy would say all this without consulting her. Endless sessions with therapists and counsellors had set time lines for swapping back the boys before they'd reached the age of 30 months. That time was long past.

At no stage, says Megs, had Sandy expressed a desire to adopt Gavin. She hadn't even requested access to him. Nor was he interested in seeing her.

Now Sandy was quoted as saying that although she loved Robin, he must go back to his real mother. At this point, according to the article, five-year-old Robin entered the room, wanting to spend some time on his mother's lap before she 'disappeared' again.

> 'Who's your Mommy?' Sandy asked
> 'You are,' he answered without hesitation.
> 'And who's your other Mommy?'
> 'Megs,' he answered.
> 'And your granny?'
> 'Joan.'
> Joan is Megs' mother.

Sandy told *YOU* she explained this to Robin often to prepare him for the return to his real mother. She was tired of Megs looking over her shoulder to check if she was bringing him up properly.

> 'I'm not one to be too concerned with what others think but now that I know I'm raising someone else's child, I'm permanently tense about Robin. I'm paranoid about his manners. It's sometimes so bad I've smacked him for not saying please or thank you.'

Sandy said she planned to start a new life in Bloemfontein with her OWN children. She made no mention of the other child she was carrying:

> 'Robin belongs with Megs in Pietermaritzburg with her own family; his granny and his grandpa who'll love and cherish him … It won't be easy, but I just have to go through with it.'

Then she was quoted as saying something that to Megs sounded like a veiled threat:

> 'It makes me angry that I just can't walk in and take my own child back. After all, according to law, Gavin is mine. I carried him for nine months. I want the judge to decide in court that we both get our biological sons back.'

Megs felt a sense of rising panic. She realised she now had to get Gavin to understand the story of his birth, before every mother at his pre-school had read the *YOU* and believed it.

She still gets tearful, 25 years later, when she remembers his little face crumpling up in confusion: 'Something died inside Gavin that day. He became distrusting. He had to hear from his own mother that she could do nothing to change the accident of his birth ... to watch a child you love have his whole world blow up around him is the most heart-rending experience. It changed Gavin for life. As an adult, he takes relationships to a certain level only. He will decide how far a relationship goes – and it will never be 100 per cent.'

After he'd been told, Joan noted a change in his behaviour. She jotted it down in a notebook she kept in the hallway near her phone landline:

> *31/10/94*: 'Megs reports while putting Gavin and friend Shaun to bed Gavin told Shaun: this is my mother and I'll NEVER leave her ...'

> '...Megs has had several talks with Gavin re swap. He asked should he go back to Sandy? Megs said what do you want to do? Stay with you. Megs told him she'd always keep him. He was number 1 with her.'

Sandy didn't get what all the fuss was about. She'd sat Robin down when he was four and told him he would have to go back to Megs sooner or later and that Gavin would have to come back to her.

'I told him it wasn't that I didn't love him, it's just that he be-longed to Megs. He knew exactly what was going on,' she says.

YOU published a follow-up article a week after the first one, on 3 November 1994:

Last week *YOU* told how Sandy Dawkins of Johannesburg whom Robin has grown up thinking of as his mother, is now pining for her biological son Gavin …

This time the journalist spoke to a psychologist who said it would have been easier for the children if they'd been swapped back at 22 months when the mistake was first discovered. They would have suffered a lot less damage because they would've still been young enough to adapt to a new mother. But at the time the mothers had been too shocked and vulnerable to be separated from their babies.

Sandy is quoted as saying: 'I love Robin, but blood is thicker than water. I want my own child back – the child I felt kicking in my womb, my firstborn, the one I talked to during the pregnancy and who looks so much like his sister.'

No, said the psychologist, blood was not always thicker than water: 'You can't swap kids like cars … from a child's point of view his "real mother" isn't necessarily the one who gave birth to him, but the one who gives him security and love and with whom he has bonded.'

YOU readers added their comments:

Lettie of Beaufort-West: 'I am so sorry for the mothers. It must have been a terrible shock when they found out the truth. Maybe they would have been better off if they'd never discovered the mistake.'

Erina of Durbanville: 'A mother puts her child first, not herself.'

Heartbroken from Bloemfontein: 'Sandy as a childless woman my advice to you is to be profoundly grateful for what you have received. There are many people who would cut off their arms for a child, no matter whose child he really was.'

Looking back, 20 years later, Sandy says she didn't do the *YOU* article to hurt Megs, although she had 'had her in chunks'.

'I felt like I was always being judged by her and I honestly didn't know what my emotions were from one day to the next. She wanted to see Robin all the time, but made excuses when I wanted to see Gavin. I felt like she was invading my privacy, I couldn't do anything without her or her mum wanting to know about it.'

As for her pregnancy, this had nothing to do with Megs, she says. Or anyone. Prior to moving the children to Bloem, they'd been living on a farm near Kliprivier and Sandy had a relationship with a man called Johan, who lived there too. She hadn't planned on getting pregnant.

But she had – and unable to cope with no money and two small children, she'd sent them away. Leaving five-year-old Robin puzzled...

Much later, he recalled, 'I can remember Kay's sister coming to the house and picking us up. As we got onto the highway I asked to have a wee and they said no. On the way I thought – why am I going to Bloem if I have another mother, Megs?'

... And Megs wondering at her strange behaviour, as Joan wrote down in her notebook:

'*7/11/94*: Megs phoned Sandy with invitation to come for Christmas. She agreed children would come at the beginning of December.

'*15/12/94*: The children didn't come.

'*3/2/95*: Megs phoned Sandy re boys' birthday on the 17th and told her a friend had seen her in a Johannesburg shopping centre. Letting her know she knew she wasn't in Bloem and that she knew she was pregnant.

'*10/2/95*: Megs phoned Sandy – are you coming? No, the children have German measles. Yet same night Gwen Smith told me the children were very well and have been ever since they've been living with her. Robin has had no sign of asthma …

'*21/3/95*: Megs phoned Robin. He said he hadn't seen Sandy for a long time. Megs mentioned Sandy's pregnancy to Gwen who acted ignorant, but she confirmed they hadn't seen her in ages.'

Robin recalls the months in Bloemfontein as the worst of his life. He hated Gwen's teenage stepsons, who he says bullied him and picked on him. And Gwen didn't sound particularly keen on having two extra children. She told *YOU*: 'I wasn't prepared just to help Sandy out whenever it suited her. We looked after the children for too long and shouldered too many of her responsibilities.'

Megs made a decision. She and John would go and fetch Robin

to stay with them until Sandy had got her act together. They told Gwen they were coming to Bloemfontein:

'John and I packed the van and were going to leave in the morning. I phoned my mom to confirm the arrangements. Then at 3 am we received a message not to come as Kay was on her way. Whether it was my call to my mother that had been listened in on, or whether Gwen had got cold feet we will never know.'

Robin remembers the day they left: 'They rushed us away from Bloem and took us to Johannesburg. We hadn't seen Sandy for months, but it felt like years to me. No one told us what was going on. Kay fetched us and we went straight to the hospital. I remember crying because I thought Sandy was dying. Meantime she'd had a Caesarean. I found out years later.'

Back in Maritzburg, Megs now had no idea where Robin was. Desperate, she phoned the bank again. Was Sandy back at work? All the supervisor knew was that she'd given birth to a son at the end of March.

It took another month before Megs got hold of Kay and left a message for Sandy to phone her, which she did the following day.

When Megs asked how the baby was, Sandy said she'd given him up for adoption. Megs was speechless with rage.

'She'd diverted her other children so that she could have a third illegitimate child and give it up for adoption without them – or anyone – knowing. The fact that she can willingly give up her natural child and deny me any access to mine – to whom she was not even providing a home – is beyond any logical explanation and I greatly resent her for it.'

It's something Megs has been unable to forget. More than ten years later, she brought it up with *60 Minutes* during one of their many update interviews, this time over a weekend at Sun City. But Sandy asked the producer not to include it in the story, leaving Megs feeling even more resentful.

'Somehow I always felt like I came across like a bit of a bully in the Australia media because of my insistence on access to Robin. By excluding all the controversial info about Sandy, they made me feel as if my concerns were petty. Her feelings were protected; mine were misrepresented.'

Megs addressed the problem with a psychologist who told her it was much easier to give up a child before you'd bonded with it, despite blood ties, especially if you never intended keeping it. But Megs could not bring herself to understand. The adoption of Sandy's third child had a profound effect on her.

Sandy has come to regret the unwanted pregnancy, but now says it didn't mean she didn't keenly feel the loss of Gavin and the affects of the swap. The judge said in court that she gave up her third child because of the uncertainty of the situation and because she was depressed and could not make commitments – he understood, so why couldn't Megs, and why still carry on about it after years after the fact?

'She should mind her own business ... I gave up my child and sent Rob and Jess to Gwen because I couldn't cope. If I'd sent Robin to Megs I would never have got him back.'

Sandy named her new son Joshua and says he went to a loving couple.

'I was very upset to give him up,' she says, 'but told his parents they should not let him know he was adopted ... I still think about him, he would be 20 now.'

Megs never forgave Sandy, but knew she had to maintain a

relationship with her in order to see Robin. But she says Sandy continued hedging, and that every time she got her hopes up to see Robin they were dashed, causing unbelievable heartache and anger.

Jeff recalls lengthy phone calls from Megs, sometimes under the weather, offloading about Sandy, with whom he maintained contact. Cell phones weren't widely used in the early nineties and contact had to be through him, Kay, or Sandy's work. It was sometimes hard even to figure out where she and the children were living.

Joan found out from Gwen that Sandy had returned to work at the bank and with Robin and Jessica was living with her sister, a police sergeant, in an 11th-floor flat at the Jeppe Police Barracks.

In May 1995, Joan noted that Robin was at pre-primary school in Bez Valley. 'Gwen said children at school in Bloem teased Robin about the swap,' she wrote. 'I told her to tell him he must laugh at them and tell them he's special and lucky to have two mothers + "Mommy Gwen".'

Joan's notebook later in the year reflects how closely Gavin was being observed in the Clinton-Parker household:

> 'Gavin's teacher noted a deterioration in Gavin's school work. Asked if any problems at home. Megs reports he has been asking questions about why and how the swap took place. I told Gavin if he was worried about something he has a choice of people to speak to — Mom, Granny, Granddad, Auntie Pat. He said: "What if it's something I can't ask anyone?" And refused to elucidate. We watched him and he seems to now have returned to normal.'

★

After eight months in Jeppestown, Sandy, Robin and Jessica moved to a flat in Southdowns, near Alberton.

Robin remembers snippets of his time there: 'I used to get really bored, so invented this secret life. Once I pretended to be camping and lit a candle in my cupboard. My clothes caught fire. I frantically tried to kill the flames, but the smell was everywhere. Sandy freaked out. I remember Jess crying and crying while she thrashed me with a pink slipper … my bottom was red for days, I could hardly sit.'

Sandy remembers the incident too: 'It was raining, I'd fallen asleep. When I woke up it was so quiet and the whole place smelled like air freshener. He'd set fire to a brand new pair of denims. I gave him a helluva hiding and for a while after that he didn't go near matches.'

Robin says Sandy's behaviour was erratic: 'She would just lose it sometimes for no reason. Once she came into my room late at night, threw everything out of my cupboard and told me I must tidy it.'

Sandy admits she had a short fuse: 'It happened that I would give him a hiding then feel sorry about it for hours afterwards. Then we'd sit together on the bed and I'd cry my eyes out because I'd hit him when he hadn't deserved it.'

She said she often felt tired and frustrated because she couldn't provide for her children. And she hated the way Megs and Joan assumed the worst of her and the company she kept.

When he was 11, Robin jumped off the roof and broke his foot. Sandy told him not to tell Megs.

'I was scared to tell her,' she says. 'Eventually I didn't want to tell her anything because she would use it as ammunition. I felt like I wasn't good enough to bring up her child. Even though I told myself what happened to him under my roof should be my business. I remember when he had his tonsils out I didn't tell her either, otherwise she would've wanted to have him assessed by her doctor first.'

Robin felt the pressure.

'There were so many things I wasn't allowed to talk about when I was little,' he said. 'It was "don't tell Megs this, don't tell Megs that". Eventually I didn't know what was fact or fiction.'

Robin had been a sickly baby, with constant colds, chest infections and colic. At six months, he was admitted to hospital with bronchial pneumonia. Later he developed asthma. Sandy had composed a document for Richard Stretch setting out her expenses to the court:

> The cost involved in rearing my child to date has been a fair amount, if taken into account doctors' consultations, hospitalisation when necessary, medication, equipment to aid his asthmatic condition, the cost not being of importance, BUT the anxiety of wondering: *Who else in his family has the same condition? How serious is this? Will he outgrow his asthma?*

Megs' grandmother had been asthmatic. She'd found the humidity in KZN so bad for her condition that they'd spent the summer months at Kestell in the Free State, where the air was much drier than the Natal Midlands.

Sandy was pleased the asthma had nothing to do with her. In her mind, the Clinton-Parker family blamed her for any perceived 'defect' in either of the children – the one she was raising and the one she'd given birth to.

★

Megs says that at no time did they ever accuse Sandy of being a bad mother. 'Our concerns were about education and stimulation and that Robin had a stable home. We wanted Sandy to have job security. And we didn't realise that she was stressing about what we thought of the day-to-day things of bringing up a kid. We didn't sweat the small stuff, but I tried to keep her informed. The point was to share the good and the bad.'

Megs had caught Gavin smoking behind her back. She wanted to tell Sandy, so phoned her up, trying to make a joke of it. Sandy saw it as criticism.

'I mean, can you believe it, Megs once phoned me when she caught Gavin smoking as a teenager and said: "Your son smokes!" Suddenly he was mine. I said to her: "Maybe he smokes, but you're busy bringing him up … you broke it girl, you fix it…"'

Megs' reaction: 'Sandy, who once appreciated my sense of humour, missed the irony of my comment. It does point to the deterioration of our relationship and the paranoia that the switch had created.'

Sandy began building up a fear of the Clinton-Parkers. Since early days, she says, the thought of a get-together with Megs and family had been enough to make her physically ill from stress: 'When we went away for that weekend at the Mount Nelson with the Aussies when the boys were 11, I had laryngitis for three months afterwards.'

Megs protests that she always looked forward to seeing Sandy: 'I didn't dislike her as a person even though I disapproved of things she did. If I had something to say, I would say it. The only reason things were brought up years later was because we kept getting asked about them in interviews.'

Sandy wasn't keen on Robin going to Megs too often because he 'behaved like a brat' when he got back:

'When he came back from Pietermaritzburg he had this un-believable attitude. It took weeks to get him back in line. They had a negative influence on him,' she says.

'Of course,' says Megs, 'that was because we had Robin in the holidays. We never had to check on his homework, or make him go to school. It was like any other divorced couple. One parent gets the short end of the stick.'

Jeff Parsons remembers phoning Robin one Christmas when he was staying with Megs.

'I said: "Happy Christmas my boy, it's your Dad." And he im-mediately said: "You are not my father." He was five. It hurt so much.'

For Robin, holidays in Pietermaritzburg meant fun. Stepfather John had had an unhappy marriage, his wife walking out on him with his young daughter. He loved the family life Megs' boys pro-vided him. He would take them drag racing, or camping. He had a bass boat, which they sometimes fished from at Albert Falls Dam.

There were some memorable occasions, says John: 'I remem-ber Robin's first fish – he was about six years old. I showed him how to put the worm on the hook, the rod was in the water for five minutes and he got a bite. A one-and-a-half kg carp! He ran up to the clubhouse to show Megs, shouting in excitement, the fish dragging behind him ...'

★

As he got older, Robin expected to spend every holiday with his biological mother. They spoke daily. She eventually gave him a cell phone and communication became much easier. They chatted about everything, from stuff he was making – he was good at building things – to the next holiday he planned to spend in Pietermaritzburg.

It irked Sandy, who didn't have the money to give Robin stuff. 'When Megs got him a cell phone, I felt like my privacy was being invaded,' she complained, 'because everything was reported to her.'

John admits that, at times, it must have seemed like they were using tactics to make life in Pietermaritzburg seem more attractive to Robin.

'We bought Gavin a 50cc quad bike, which made Robin green when he saw it. So we bought one for Robin too ... But obviously he couldn't take it home to Sandy because he always came by bus. It was for when he came to see us in Pietermaritzburg.'

After a holiday of fishing, biking, TV games and get-togethers with the extended Clinton-Parker family, Robin would go home to Daleside, a forlorn, economically depressed settlement in Randvaal with not unpleasant views of the Suikerbosrand Nature Reserve. They lived there with Kay, Sandy's mother.

These days, looking back, Robin describes the area as a 'shithole' and has few good memories.

'It was boring and we never had money. Not once or twice, many times, I would be sent to the neighbours to charm them into giving us cash to buy food. R50 here, R50 there. I always promised that Sandy would pay them back, but she never did.'

Sandy says he has it wrong and that she actually sent him to extract payment from the neighbours for stealing electricity from them. Whatever the case, things were tight. Robin as an adult is money conscious, often in debt and not shy to ask for a loan.

'Money is power,' he says. 'My wife even says to me, you make money a god. Sandy was always saying: "One day when I have money." I inherited a few things from her – like her short temper and money issues.'

Because Sandy lived in what Robin calls 'one day land', he says he often felt the need to help her get on her feet, even when he was only 11 or 12.

'I heard from a friend's dad about a company that needed a forklift driver and arranged it for Sandy. I was so excited and then so disappointed when she didn't make a go of it.'

Sandy laughs when asked about it. 'Yeah, right, they put me on top of the forks of the fork lift and dumped me onto a truck to offload sand. Of course I couldn't do it.'

The point, says Robin, is that Sandy seemed unable to better herself, or gain the confidence to take risks.

'I just didn't get the way she operated. She just didn't grab opportunities. She waited for things to happen, rather than make them happen ... and tended to blame the swap for her life circumstances.'

★

They weren't circumstances that Gavin wanted much to do with. As a child he was anxious about leaving Megs, but as he got older he better understood the situation and realised no one was going to take his life away from him.

In his early teens, he'd spend the odd weekend with Sandy, which Megs would arrange. A talented badminton player, he travelled to Johannesburg twice for tournaments and went to stay with his biological mother, grandmother and sister. And Robin. He remembers Sandy being delighted to have him for the night, Robin less so.

'Robin got the complete shits with me. He wasn't used to sharing his space, although he shared mine when he came for holidays in Pietermaritzburg.'

Sandy couldn't help noticing the conflict: 'Robin was excessively jealous when Gavin came to stay,' she remembers. 'It was clear his nose was out of joint.'

Robin admits to feeling threatened by Gavin's visit because Sandy was all over him like a rash. Sandy says it was a tense time: 'The atmosphere was awful ... I spent the weekend in tears ... When Gavin left things didn't improve. It was almost like Robin wanted Gavin's life.'

That was exactly what Robin wanted. Gavin was living his life, with all the benefits that went with it, leaving him at a distinct disadvantage in a household that was stretched to the limits.

Sandy was at a loss about what to do with the boy she'd brought up. He hated school, didn't bother with homework and listened to her less and less.

'Robin just took his freedom and ran with it,' she says. 'I got tired of trying to control him.'

Megs too noticed that as Robin grew older he began realising that he needed to get away from Sandy.

Then something happened that gave Sandy some control back. She had a phone call from Dave Lotter's cousin, Shelley, from Pietermaritzburg.

Dave wanted to meet his son.

Dave

Sandy: 'Meeting Dave was the best thing that ever happened to Robin. I knew it would make Megs angry, but I just felt it had to happen. Robin had a right to get to know his own dad and make up his mind about it, so I allowed it.'

Megs: 'Angry? Yes it made me angry because it was dangerous. Not because he was going to meet him. There were two conditions when I gave Shelley the photograph: that Robin was not allowed to go to Zimbabwe and that there would be no more humiliating blood tests for me. He was welcome to do his own.'

★

Now in Zimbabwe, Dave and his third wife, Nikki, originally from Howick, were living in the Odzi area of Manicaland, between Harare and Mutare. They'd farmed tobacco for a while then sold up, intending to move north to Mhangura, where Dave's godmother farmed with her son. But after the land invasions began in 2000, farming in Zimbabwe came to a grinding halt. His godmother and many others lost their homes, their land and their livelihood.

Of the 105 farmers in Odzi, only seven remained. Many had fled overnight, abandoning their crops, homesteads, tractors and livestock, hiding out at Kariba, or in Zambia, hoping it would all eventually blow over.

Dave weighed up his options. Zimbabwe was in his blood; his father's brother, a professional boxer, had lived there and they'd visited him often. Although he'd grown up in Natal, he'd always wanted to return to the vast, incredible open spaces of what he felt was God's country.

He was as passionate about hunting. With its varied habitats and vegetation and abundance of wild life, Zimbabwe was prime hunting territory. Hunters would come from around the world to shoot eland, buffalo, leopard, lion and elephant and warthog. Hunting brought in much-needed foreign currency and Dave reckoned he'd survive if he could do something that had the tacit backing of government. So he'd started a hunting company, Hogs Safari, and struck a deal with local politicians. For a while was able to carry on his business without interference.

Around him, farms were being taken over by drunken unemployed youth militia who'd arrive in a truck-cloud of dust and forcibly evict the owners because a high-powered politician wanted a ready-made commercial farm, or to sub-divide it to sell plots.

In the midst of this climate of fear, Dave decided it was time to meet his third son. He'd received a letter from his busybody cousin, Shelley. Her mother and Dave's were sisters. She was also a work colleague of Megs and had got to know Robin on his visits to Pietermaritzburg.

Attached to Shelley's email was a photograph of 13-year-old Robin.

'It smacked me between the eyes,' says Dave. 'I'd seen pictures of him in magazines – usually accompanied by an article saying something dreadful about me – but when I saw this sad-looking boy in the photograph, so much like my brother, I knew I had to meet him. I had this feeling he was incredibly desperate. For a long time I had bull-shitted myself that Robin wasn't my child, because no one proved to me that he was. Now I had no doubt that he was, but the reality of the situation is that he could well not have been.'

As he grew up, Robin was becoming increasingly aware that a twist of fate had dumped him on Sandy and her family. As clinical psychologist Clive Willows had said, 'Adolescence is a time of identity formation, which is based in part on a teenager coming to terms with his roots and his identification with the history of his family. Unlike adopted children they can be given no reason as to their circumstances. There may be a need to identify more strongly with their biological families.'

Gavin, living Robin's life, had it easy, Robin thought, never having to struggle for a thing. He was always thinking: 'What would it have been like? Who would I have been?'

He was about to discover the answer to a question he'd been asking Megs for years: *What's my father like?* Megs had tried to protect him, she says, by telling him as little as possible. Dave had shown no interest in either Gavin or Robin, buggering off to Malawi, then Zimbabwe, leaving her to explain to Robin why he didn't give a damn.

Now, apparently, he did. He wrote a letter Robin has never forgotten, introducing himself as his father. He was married and his wife's name was Nikki. He lived in Zimbabwe and he was a professional hunter. And he wanted to meet his son.

★

Dave and Nikki planned to drive to Johannesburg a few days before Robin's school broke up and take him back with them for his September holidays. An unusually motivated Sandy helped him organise his passport, which had expired since the US trips to see Maury Povich. Robin remembers being surprised at Sandy's interest and enthusiasm.

'As kids, Jess and I were basically like mushrooms: kept in the dark and fed shit. Now she was helping me to go to Zim with my Dad, telling me not to tell Megs. She wanted to control things. I felt caught between her and Megs. I didn't know what to do. I wanted to tell Megs, but was scared she would say no, or that I must meet Dave on her terms – under her roof.'

Megs was hurt. 'When I'd told Dave about the test results he wasn't interested. He didn't want to know. He broke my heart and let me down at a critical point of my and his son's life. Why would I expose Robin to someone who had rejected him as a baby? I wanted to protect him from rejection.'

Dave and Nikki spent the night with friends in Johannesburg and picked up Robin the following day. Sandy remembers his excitement. 'He got up at the crack of dawn and even tidied his room, which he never normally did. He was awestruck at having a father for the first time in his life ...'

Robin wasn't disappointed.

'He arrived at the gate in a green Land Cruiser and I thought wow, how cool. He's a warm welcoming person and I felt drawn to him immediately. I was proud to have him as my dad. I couldn't stop staring at him.'

Dave and Nikki took Sandy, Robin and Jessica out to the KFC in Meyerton. Sandy's house in Daleside wasn't an option.

Dave assessed the situation at a glance: 'I realised things weren't good with Sandy when I walked in there. Looking at the house and how Rob was dressed ... We took them for coffee so she could at least get to know us before her son left with complete strangers.'

Dave was of compact build and personable like his son. There was an instant connection, says Sandy.

'Jess and I felt sad watching them together – the similarities – and I thought what an injustice Megs had done Robin by not letting him get to know his father. Robin just sat there observing his dad, not saying a lot.'

For Robin, the meeting was unforgettable: 'There was so much going through my mind. I was analysing him. I had been told that this was my father, but how did I know? I had no proof. So I kept looking for signs. I looked at his features to see if they were like mine, how he moved.'

They set off on the long road to Zimbabwe. Dave remembers things being awkward at first, with Robin trying hard to please his new father and stepmother. He was also concerned about Nikki, whom he'd now introduced to his fifth child.

Nikki had known Dave for years without being aware of Robin's existence, so the sudden appearance of a 14-year-old who couldn't take his eyes off his father – and who was as like him as peas in a pod – was a bit of a shock. She couldn't help being a little resentful at first, but after a couple of days Robin was calling her 'Mom'.

'Nikki is a loving and supportive person,' says Robin. 'She is able to see a situation from a distance and analyse it unemotionally. I feel like I can talk to her about anything and she treats me like the child she never had. But her first priority is my dad.'

★

Robin thought Hogs Safari was paradise. He wasn't a child who could sit still – ever – and now he didn't have to. He was having the time of his life with a man who liked all the same things he did and was as hyperactive.

Dave understood completely: 'Here he was in this vast incredible Zimbabwean bush and Dad is a hunter and he suddenly loves hunting; Dad rides motorbikes and Robin loves motorbikes. Every day we did something different. Either out with clients, or working with game. He was over the moon.'

Although he'd done some target shooting, Robin had never been hunting. They needed meat for the lodge, so Dave said they should leave early the next morning to go and shoot some. Rob was scared – he'd never shot with a rifle or driven a car. The next morning his father told him to get behind the wheel of the open Land Rover.

'It was very early and cold,' relates Robin. 'I didn't know how to drive, but he showed me the basics and off we went. He spotted some wild pigs in the marshes and told me to put foot. I drove straight into the marshes and the pigs scattered. He shot them one after the other.'

★

After the best fortnight of his life, Dave and Nikki drove Robin to Harare to catch a plane back to Jo'burg.

'It had been ten days in which we'd tried to catch up our whole lives,' says Robin. 'I felt like I should say something meaningful in case I never got another opportunity. I had finally found the missing piece of the puzzle in my life.'

Dave had begun to read Robin's predicament: 'He was sad when he left, but I felt he was able to handle it. I could see and read the situation he was in. I thought that I had to get him out of there, but wasn't sure how.'

Robin felt transformed: 'I knew when I got back home I had to move on from Sandy. I had found this older and wiser version of me. I didn't belong with Sandy.'

Sandy had been avoiding Megs' phone calls: 'Whenever Megs phoned during those two weeks he was away, I would lie to her and say he was at a friend's. I thought Robin needed to get to know his father. I didn't do it to spite her. I didn't do it sneakily,' she protests.

But she could not bring herself to tell Megs. It became Robin's responsibility: 'Sandy knew that Megs would be pissed off, yet left it to me to break the news to her. I was 14, but had to make all these decisions. Why couldn't Sandy pick up the phone and tell Megs?' he says.

Three months later, Robin spent Christmas with Megs in Pietermaritzburg. As it turned out, Dave and Nikki were also in KZN for Christmas. Megs had heard from Shelley that Dave had been affected after seeing the photograph she'd given her. Now she asked her why Dave was rejecting his son again. Why didn't he call? Shelley came clean and told her about the Zim trip.

Megs recalls: 'I came home and said to Robin: "Is there anything you need to tell me?" He said as a matter of fact there is. And said that Dave had told him that if he didn't tell me he was going to phone me himself. And so I found out about Sandy's betrayal. I think Sandy enjoyed defying me in her mind and not telling me.

'I was furious because I'd always wanted Robin to meet his Dad and I would like to have witnessed it. But it was all done behind my back. I had wanted so much to be part of that process. It wasn't Sandy's call to make. Contrary to what people think, I once adored Dave, he was my friend, we'd had a ball together. I know I should've been happy that Robin called Nikki "Mom" so readily, it was a reflection of her commitment to him. At the time it felt like he had replaced me. To this day I cringe if I overhear him calling her "Mom" on the phone.'

★

There was no love lost between Robin and Sandy's mother Kay, with whom they lived. Most of the time she was silent, says Robin.

'When we moved in with Kay, life became a real challenge … Kay was an introvert; I'm an extrovert. From when I was very little I used to wonder how we could be related. In the end we didn't even like each other.'

Kay may have been an introvert, says Sandy, but she wouldn't put up with Robin's backchat. He'd become rude since his return from Zimbabwe. This led to their first major and terminal fall-out, which he remembers clearly:

'I told Sandy that Kay didn't like me and she slapped me. I told her straight: "If you do that again I will punch you as hard as I can." I said to her: "I am leaving, I am going to Megs." And I started walking. I was out of the property when I heard Jessica calling after me and crying. I went back, but two weeks later I was on a bus, I was gone. Sandy tried to kiss and make up, but it was too late. I was set. She and a friend took me to the bus. She cried. I didn't.'

Thirteen years since stepping off a bus as a toddler to meet Megs for the first time, Robin arrived in Pietermaritzburg with his mind made up: there would be no return ticket.

Megs' only regret was that it had taken so long.

Checking Out

Megs: 'So in the end I got both kids, but it wasn't a triumph. It hadn't been an easy journey. There'd been lots of heartbreak along the way.'

★

When Megs got the phone call from Robin that he was leaving Sandy for good, she told no one, except John:

'I was scared to get my hopes up. It was a day I had dreamt about. I had wept for it. I had prayed for it more than anything in my life. I had thought about him every single day from the day I found out. I didn't even tell my mother until he'd arrived.'

John phoned Sandy. If Megs phoned, Sandy might feel like she'd lost the battle of her life. 'It took guts on her part and I respect her for that,' he says. 'It must've been so hard to let him go.'

Sandy seemed surprisingly accepting. She told John that Robin's heart was in Pietermaritzburg.

She told Peter Overton of *60 Minutes Australia*: 'I knew there

120

was a void in his life that needed filling and there was no ways I could fill it, and I discussed it with him. I said to him, "Think about it and give it a couple of days and we'll talk about it."

Peter Overton: 'He accepted your offer?'

Sandy: 'I promise you I was shocked, I really was shocked.'

So was Gavin, who says he wasn't consulted about the move at all. And he remembers not being particularly pleased to see Robin and his few worldly possessions entering his space full-time.

'I remember thinking: uh-oh … there goes my only child status out of the window. I hadn't minded during the holidays. But suddenly it seemed like I was going to be sacrificing a whole lot more in the foreseeable future.'

In interviews, Gavin was often made to sound like an unappreciative kid who had struck it lucky.

Peter Overton: 'Would you ever want to go and live with Sandy?'

Gavin: 'Not really. I'm happy down here.'

Peter: 'You are happy with the life you were accidentally given?'

Gavin: 'Yeah.'

Peter Overton: 'Do you feel sorry for Robin?'

Gavin: 'Not really.'

Gavin refused to be emotionally drawn into the accident of his birth. He'd grabbed the life he was given and was living it. He had nothing in common with his biological parents and they never got an opportunity to bond with him: 'They never really made an effort,' he says. 'I was the child – why was it up to me to make a plan to see them?'

Jeff says initially they tried. A telegram sent in 1995, on the day before Gavin turned six, reads:

HAPPY BIRTHDAY LOTS OF LOVE XX DAD
+ AUDREY

When Gavin turned seven, Jeff had phoned him in Pietermaritzburg. Throughout the conversation John chirped in the background about Jeff being an absent father and told Gavin to tell him if he was only going to phone once a year, he might as well not phone at all.

Sandy says John was rude and put Jeff off ever contacting his son again.

To Jeff, there was simply no connection with Gavin. He couldn't muster up interest in a child because he looked like him, walked like him, smiled like him. He felt that Gavin had been mollycoddled by Megs and couldn't relate to him the way he could to Robin and his other children. 'I wish I'd brought him up… she spoilt him rotten,' he says.

It still surprises Megs that neither Sandy nor Jeff had any desire whatsoever to bond with their biological son.

His biological sister Jessica says Sandy tried.

'Sandy once sent him a message, saying when is he coming to visit? He replied on Facebook and gave her a rocket, saying he's the kid in the situation. He slagged us all off, including Jeff. It made me furious. I don't want anything to do with him.'

Gavin remembers: 'I just got pissed off and lost it. Why couldn't they make an effort to see me? Instead it was always "when are you coming here?" I wasn't in a financial position to make it happen, just like them. I know it upset them all, but I was upset that none of them ever made an effort.'

Throughout his childhood, Gavin's comfort zone was the family that brought him up.

'Nothing in my nature comes from the Dawkins. If I'd stayed there I bet I wouldn't have finished school or left home. Megs and my gran, Joan, instilled in me a desire to do well and take responsibility for my actions. Nothing of me, except my receding hairline and some other physical features, comes from Jeff and Sandy.'

Both boys believe they've inherited Megs' temperament.

'I have the same stubborn craziness as my mother...' claims Robin.

Gavin concurs: 'I have Megs' temper – if I lose it, I lose it. And like her, with me it's "Fool me once, shame on you. Fool me twice, shame on me."'

Gavin grew up aware of the huge gap in Megs' life, caused by her absent biological son, but also knowing that he was the constant one, her anchor.

Megs admits that when Robin was around for holidays, Gavin came second.

'I could see Gav, nurture him, protect him any day I liked,' she says, 'but I couldn't do the same for Robin … he was mine, but he wasn't mine.'

Now it was time to level the playing fields. But it turned out to be a lot more difficult than any of them had imagined. Fifteen years of living with Sandy had shaped Robin's attitude to education and discipline.

He had attended Hoërskool DF Malan in Meyerton in the Vaal and hadn't been a star pupil. He arrived in Pietermaritzburg with a note from the principal informing his parents that their child had failed his mid-year Grade 9 exams.

No big deal to Sandy, who'd left school before finishing and would later allow Jessica to quit too. Sandy says Jessica fell to pieces after Robin left home, which is why she allowed her to leave. But she'd resisted a good education for Robin too. Megs' sister Kit had offered to have him to stay with them so that he could attend Marais Viljoen in Alberton, a technical school.

Robin says: 'It was a really good school and Auntie Kit was prepared to pay for everything. But Sandy told her I was already at a technical school, which wasn't true. She just said anything to keep me.'

So under the misapprehension that Robin had been attending a vocational school, Megs and John enrolled him at Linpark High in Pietermaritzburg, where he could do technical subjects.

Technically Robin was as sharp as a button, commented John, who once came home to find that he'd stripped the lawn mower and was putting it back together.

Robin repeated Grade 9 in 2005, doing well in nothing except Afrikaans.

Maths – 35%
Natural Science – 35%
Arts & Culture – 34%
English – 40%
Afrikaans – 72%

Megs puts it partly down to him being thrust into an English environment after years of Afrikaans tuition, not easy in subjects like Maths and Science. She also believes he wasn't stimulated enough as a child.

Sandy rolls her eyes: 'Megs actually once phoned me up as if it was my fault he was failing. She said "I can understand why he's doing so badly because you were useless at maths." If it was Gavin, it was a family weakness, if it was Robin it was the way I'd brought him up.'

Megs says she'd merely been trying to involve Sandy after Robin had left, because she made no attempt to contact him. Or Gavin.

'Robin phoned her initially after he arrived,' she says. 'He made an effort to keep contact. I told him I wouldn't stop him, but shouldn't SHE be contacting HIM?'

Sandy was dismissive: 'What does she expect? She's ruined my life. I don't have a son any more. Jessica doesn't have a brother. For years I had to watch Gavin growing up through her because Megs brainwashed him into not seeing me.'

Megs disagrees: 'If she had an issue with me, what stopped her contacting him? Problem was I bonded with Robin when he was little; she did not bond with Gavin.'

Robin was frustrated: 'I felt I owed it to Sandy to keep contact. She'd brought me up. But I did all the work. She never contacted me. I didn't get why she didn't make an effort. Just a message would've been nice.'

Sandy says she thought about Robin all the time after he left. She'd be walking in the street and would imagine the person in front of her was him, then realise it couldn't be. She would dream about him. But she didn't contact him, deciding instead to leave him to 'get on with it'.

When *60 Minutes* returned to do the latest development, for the first time the four of them didn't get together. Megs was interviewed in Pietermaritzburg, Sandy in Johannesburg.

Peter Overton spoke to Sandy: 'So you reckon she's completely dudded you?' he probed.

> Sandy: 'For sure, for sure. I mean she made no bones about it from the start that she wanted both boys. How she managed to manipulate that I have no clue.'

> Peter: 'You say Megs has manipulated the boys? Bribed the boys?'

> Sandy: 'Definitely. I don't think it … I know it. I know it.'

Megs had always made it clear she wanted both boys.

Megs: 'I'm not even going to try to deny that. I don't know that I've manipulated it. I've always said from the beginning that it was my intention to get them both because I needed that to survive.'

Peter: 'You ended up with everything.'

Megs: 'I know, and I'm chuffed about it. Of course I'm chuffed about it.'

Sandy: 'Oh I hope she's happy, I really do, because my honest answer on that one is – like she always said to me – she told people there's a bus out there with my name on it. Whatever I've done, it can't be that bad. But best she just be careful because that bus is making a U-turn and it's got her name on it now.'

The story got heated responses from Channel 9 viewers back in Australia. Megs, who only read them years later on Facebook, felt hurt, because they all felt sorry for Sandy. She was shocked that they thought she could support two families. And hated that they criticised the boys:

Nb97 If Megs really cared about her son she could've given him financial support and allowed him to stay with his own mother – that is the mother who raised him. She was really only thinking of her own needs...

TammieB What Megs did was selfish and cruel ... she had the means to give this child a better life without taking him away from his mother. Robin must be some kind of an emotional cripple to be able to turn his back on the woman who loved him since birth, all in the name of prosperity.

Petal I thought Gavin came across as a smug unsympathetic character. Why doesn't he go and see his birth mother, just as, you know, a kind of gesture?

LaLaLauren It is horrible that Sandy was left with nothing. Gavin did nothing to try and have a relationship with his bio-mother and has clearly no interest in her 'less fortunate' life.

shelikestowrite Wow poor Sandy. Seems like this story brings up how much we value wealth and material possessions. There are so many other wonderful situations where biology means nothing when it comes to family, such as adoption, step parents, foster parents.

Teacup This is incredibly sad. I wonder how much 60 Minutes, with its revisiting them repeatedly, altered the outcome of the story? There seemed to be quite an emphasis placed on the disparity of economic status. It doesn't take much for seeds of envy to grow.

Lizi Your point about the effect of the 60 Minutes visits is really interesting. In particular, I felt quite uncomfortable with the questions Peter Overton was asking Gavin at age 15, trying to make him feel guilty about living a life he'd had no choice about living.

What Sandy and her supporters didn't know was that things weren't exactly blissful in Pietermaritzburg. Megs and John found themselves in a war zone.

'So there we were with two boys in their teens and not at all pleased to be in the same place,' John recalled. 'Gavin was used to having the house to himself. He was used to being the top dog.'

Robin felt Gavin had lived his life for long enough. Now it was his turn to benefit.

'When we were little it was fine. I would come for holidays and he would share for a week or two. Then I went and it was all his again. Now I sort of felt, well, I'm here and now it's my turn because you've had 15 years of my mum and she's actually mine, you know. We basically hated each other.'

Gavin was intensely aware of the complications. 'It's the biological son of the person that you love the most,' he says, 'so you don't know if you're going to be forgotten about or not.'

Megs' sister Pat watched from the sidelines: 'They would wind each other up to see who mum loved best, to see who would come out on top. It was so competitive. I thought they would eventually get used to each other.'

Thankfully, says Gavin, Robin wasn't at the same school as him: 'At least we had separate lives and I didn't have to be responsible for his behaviour. Linpark was a trade school, low LSM. New kid Robin arrives and starts shooting his mouth off, as he does. He had a daredevil streak and would think nothing of taking on the meanest kid at school, even though he was half the size.'

When Robin was 16, John bought him got a Hyosung 125 on-off road scrambler.

Robin remembers: 'I used to clean John's workshop for him, then he started trusting me on the machines. I once spent a whole three-week holiday working there. He didn't pay me, but said he would make it up to me. He eventually bought me a motorbike.'

To Robin it meant freedom, even though he didn't have a licence: 'Megs would take Gavin to school and John used to take me. One day he couldn't, so he told me to go on my bike. From then on I just did my own thing. It was convenient for John and no one ever asked questions.'

Gavin would look on, bemused, as Robin vanished with a noisy rev: 'Robin would just disappear, like he had at Sandy's. He'd thought life with us would be one long comfortable holiday, but Megs expected him to study during the week and catch up all the schoolwork he'd missed out on. I was ahead of him at school, but would still tell everyone where I was going to be.'

In Grade 10, Robin moved to Carter High School, where Gavin was in his matric year. Robin laughs when he remembers parents' evenings at Carter: 'Everyone used to praise Gavin, then when they got to me it was like "Hehe – we gotta talk, my boy"... Gavin was such a goody-goody it used to drive me mad. I would hide my report; he'd be showing his off.'

The general comments in a typical Gavin report would read: 'Gavin is actively involved in the student life of the school and is unfailingly charming and polite ... Gavin has participated in swimming and badminton and was a library monitor for the first two terms of this year. He has a strong sense of civic duty and displays energy and initiative. His work ethic is commendable.'

Robin's work ethic, everyone agreed, was anything but commendable. From having freedom at Sandy's, albeit with financial constraints, he had stepped into an organised household. He was expected to go to school every day and be home at a certain hour.

'Megs was like a policewoman,' he recalled ruefully, 'wanting to know where I was all the time. I understand now that I have kids, but I didn't then.'

His aunt Pat found him a curious mix. Genetically he was Clinton-Parker; the way he talked and behaved often wasn't: 'He'd say things like he had food stuck on his "pelmet" – meaning palate,' she recalled. 'Megs used to moan at him a lot about his table manners and about things like using a knife and fork. Stuff Gavin had grown up with.'

The situation in the household reminded them of the AA Milne poem:

> There were two little Bears, who lived in a Wood,
> And one of them was Bad and the other was Good.
> Good Bear learnt his Twice Times One –
> But Bad Bear left all his buttons undone.
>
> They lived in a tree when the weather was hot,
> And one of them was Good, and the other was not.
> Good Bear learnt his Twice Times Two –
> But Bad Bear's thingummies were worn right through.

Gavin swam for the first team and played badminton for Kwa-Zulu Natal and SA Country Districts. He'd do his homework and his chores without fuss.

Robin would leave John's tools lying out in the rain, forget to clean up the dog pooh and had no clue how to study: 'I just couldn't study. I tried. Gavin was used to all that stuff. Megs didn't get that I could spend the whole weekend trying to go through schoolwork and it just didn't penetrate my brain.'

But he knew exactly how to irritate Gavin. Gavin didn't want Robin in his room, a request Robin didn't respect. They had punch-ups when Robin helped himself to Gavin's things. Robin thought Gavin was a selfish city boy; Gavin thought Robin was a slacker.

John tried to get the boys to resolve their differences: 'I got them together one day, told them all to keep quiet - then gave Robin ten minutes to air his grievances, then Gavin. It was all about turf and territory. And curfews. Robin wanted the same treatment as Gavin, even when Gavin was at college and he was still at school. He couldn't understand there were different rules for schoolboys.'

Robin remembers: 'I felt it was stupid that I had to go to bed at ten o'clock and not him just because he was ahead of me at school. I was the firstborn.'

Robin also began to resent John, who he felt was much stricter with him than he was with Gavin. He felt he was always being told to do things.

'Gavin was wise to John,' he says. 'He would tell him to go and make his own coffee. At first I didn't mind helping, but then I got sick of running around after him.'

Pat remembers too: 'When we came to visit, before we even knew Robin was in the house, we'd hear John shouting: R-o-o-bi-i-ii-iiiin!'

John thought Robin needed disciplining; Megs supported him, to Robin's disgust.

'The rules of the house are not new to you,' she wrote in a letter to him. 'Perhaps during a holiday they were a novelty but they were always there. Everyone has chores growing up – EVERYONE – unless you were born with a golden spoon in your mouth. We are getting you the best education that we can afford – you need to come to the party and show some courtesy, assistance and general decency.'

Robin felt stifled.

'They were always setting boundaries for me,' he recalls. 'For years I'd longed to be with Megs, then after three years I couldn't stand it. There was way too much control. When I am constantly under pressure you are going to turn me into a dragon. It's not who I am. It was like I was in a bottle and the lid was closed.'

It was at this point that Dave re-entered their lives.

After Megs

Things had become untenable in parts of Zimbabwe. Zanu-PF had won another election and although seen as a rare chance to pull the country back from the brink, the politicisation of land-related injustices had again been the rallying cry. The prices of food and fuel had sky-rocketed because of drought and the cha-otic land redistribution programme. Commercial white farmers were now an endangered species, the numbers having dropped from 5 000 to 500. Dave had survived in the hunting industry by doing deals and forming strategic partnerships. But he was getting tired of playing games and couldn't continue paying off police and local politicians in money, meat and mealie-meal.

The tipping point was when he and his second son, Clive, were taken to the Odzi police station and beaten up.

'Things were rotting out and there was no rule of law,' he says. 'We couldn't carry on paying off people who weren't very nice at all, so with heavy hearts, we left.'

In 2005 they returned to the Howick area, less than half an hour's drive from Pietermaritzburg. Robin was delighted to be reunited with his father and they caught up easily. Dave would fetch him for lunch, or for the weekend. He'd wait outside the house, avoiding contact with Megs if he could. Megs stayed inside, for the same reason.

It became clear to Dave that Robin was increasingly fed up with the confines of his new life. He complained to family and to some of his friends' parents that it was like boot camp, that John ordered him around non-stop and Megs expected too much of him. He told Dave that Gavin was gay and on drugs and that he couldn't live in the same house as him (though according to Megs Robin didn't share this with her).

Today Megs has the following to say: 'I was upset that Robin hadn't approached me. Instead he went to Dave and to family friends and bad-mouthed Gavin. Gav was a top badminton player and took supplements. He certainly wasn't on drugs. To me this was a big betrayal. He tried to make Gavin look especially bad in Dave's eyes. I believed it was insecurity in his new relationship with his father. I don't believe Robin was concerned about Gavin's well-being.'

Dave remembers the day. 'One afternoon he phoned me in a state and said he wanted me to come and fetch him. Nikki and I went round and everyone was upset.'

'It was terrible,' says Robin. 'Dad and Nikki on one couch, John and Megs on the other. Half of me was thinking: how on earth did Mum and Dave ever get together? They are so different. The other half of me thought: okay, here's an opportunity to sort all this *kak* out.'

As Dave recalls, 'Rob went off about the way John was always shitting on him and that Megs couldn't see how she favoured

Gavin over him. He thought that Gavin and John had, at his expense, benefited from the money made from the publicity about the swap. She'd even bought John a new workshop.'

Megs didn't bother to defend herself against what she felt were ludicrous accusations being made by a manipulative 16-year-old. She and John had taken out a separate bond to buy the machines for the workshop. He was her husband and she was entitled to support him, as he had done her. She told Dave his son was full of shit and jumping to conclusions about matters he knew nothing of. If he wanted to go and live with Dave, then she wouldn't stop him.

'Rob had told me he wanted to go and stay with his dad, but I didn't think he would actually go,' she says. 'By the time Dave arrived to pick him up there wasn't much more to say. I was exhausted by then.'

She told Robin to go and pack his things. Dave remembers carrying Robin's fishing rods to the car, while Megs stood on the verandah watching.

Dave says that when Robin tried to take the motorbike he'd got from Megs and John, she stopped him and told him he should walk out exactly the way he'd walked in from Sandy – with nothing.

According to Megs, 'He took all his stuff, including his moto-X bike that he had bought with the money he got from the Australian *60 Minutes* interviews. But when he tried to take the road bike we'd bought him, I stopped him. He was leaving his life with us and I didn't think it was okay to take with him all the trappings of that life if it was so awful.'

After packing the vehicle, Rob went back to the house and gave her a hug.

'I died inside – I died,' says Megs. 'I can't tell you, it hurt so much. Because I had fought so hard for him, I wanted him so much and then it failed. It had never occurred to me that it would fail. I wanted all the right things for the right reasons, but they just didn't fit into place.'

What made the departure worse was that Joan, her anchor, had passed away the previous year.

'I missed my mum immensely and longed for her comfort and advice. If she'd been alive she would never have allowed him to leave. She would have sorted something out.'

The first person Megs phoned was Pat, who thought something dreadful must've happened to Robin.

'She was howling her eyes out. She couldn't speak she was crying so much. She sobbed: he's gone ... he's gone ... I said *who's gone?* I went straight over to their house. John shot of out the door; he couldn't take it. I just sat with her and she talked and talked. The problem was that she hadn't seen it coming, she had no idea he was thinking of moving out, or going to live with Dave.'

'We'd invested in Robin and suddenly he was gone,' says John. 'I was left with Megs who was in a state. Gavin didn't show that it bugged him that Robin had left. They had fought about everything, even the remote for the TV.'

Gavin acted indifferent: 'Just as he walked out on Sandy, now he walked out on Megs ... and probably wondered why we didn't chase after him.'

Robin denies this: 'I didn't wonder that at all. I would've gone anyway. Dave just felt like the best option. If he hadn't been there I would have made another plan.'

When Robin phoned Megs for Mother's Day a few weeks later, she cut him dead.

'I was like a zombie and here he was phoning me for Mother's Day like nothing had happened,' she says.

'I just wanted to wish her for that day,' protests Robin. 'I wanted her to be happy on that special day, despite our issues. You can fight with me tomorrow. But she was like a cold fish.'

'Megs can be very irrational,' conceded John. 'When you hurt her, she takes it very badly. Robin was one of the loves of her life and he took a huge chunk out of her heart.'

Megs wrote Robin a letter, addressing what she thought of as his betrayal of her family and his accusations that Gavin took drugs. It was a letter she never posted.

> I thought about you every single day from the day that I found out about you. Only when you came to live here did I start feeling whole again. You had your freedom, you had love, but you threw it all away and betrayed us. And betrayed Gavin. If you were worried about his welfare, as you told your Dad, you could've gone to Aunty Pat. Gavin may forgive you for betraying him, but he will not forgive you for betraying me. Betrayal this deep does not disappear overnight. Ultimately the real loser is you.

Gavin echoed his mother when he spoke to *60 Minutes* in 2012.

> Gavin: 'For me, if you hurt someone that I care about, I will either kill you or you get the hell away from us – so...'

Peter Overton: 'Why did you feel you want to kill him?'

Gavin: 'It was the fact that he hurt Megs. She felt really hurt and extremely betrayed when he walked out. She'd given him a home – given him everything and he walked out throwing everything at us.'

Robin: 'For me to try and change in 2–3 years to keep Megs happy was hard. I tried and I thought I could do it, but I couldn't.'

That he walked out with Dave didn't help Megs forgive him: 'I can't believe that you were so willing to give up something we had worked so hard to achieve, for someone who had betrayed your mother, ignored you your whole life and had lied his way into your heart,' she wrote.

One of the first things Rob did on leaving Megs was to quit school. Dave agreed it was probably the best option.

Megs was not impressed when Carter High phoned to find out where her son was. She assumed Dave had found it too much of an inconvenience to take Robin to school in Maritz-burg every day.

She wrote in the unsent letter that her brother and cousins had also hated school 'but every single one of them finished school because they knew it was important for them and their parents… You had your freedom, you had love and everything that you needed. All we asked for in return was courtesy, assistance and to work hard at school.'

Dave felt he'd done the right thing by taking Robin out of

school – although, says Sandy, he phoned her to ask her advice, which she found curious.

'I asked him why he was phoning me and not Megs. He said, "well, you brought him up; you know what makes him tick".'

Sandy assumed Dave didn't want Megs calling the shots anymore. Megs would never see reason when it came to education.

Dave says he eventually did what felt right.

'Robin was angry and desperate for things he didn't have in life. He felt school was standing in his way. He was good at practical stuff. So I hooked him up with a taxidermist friend – and he did an apprenticeship with him in Howick.'

Robin thrived at the Academy of Taxidermy, run by Australian, Tony Psaila. He too had left school before finishing and started working in the family business in Australia. In 2001, having seen a gap in the market in South Africa, Psaila moved to Howick. Under him, Robin learnt how to skin animals, preserve hides, mount birds, boil skulls and pack trophies for export. There's a picture of him with other students on the academy website, putting the finishing touches to the mane of a menacing-looking, but very dead lion. The skin belonged to a hunter and the students had stretched it over a manikin made from polyurethane. In another picture Robin lies next to a crocodile, its jaws stretched wide in a deathly grimace, as he concentrates on replacing its teeth.

Jeff, looking at a picture of Robin smiling next to a dead impala, shudders when he thinks of the sweet little boy who was once his son, shooting and stuffing animals.

'He was always comfortable with guns and good with his hands,' he says. 'He used to draw stuff and discuss with me how to make whatever it was he'd designed.'

★

Gavin had enrolled to study hotel management at Varsity College in Maritzburg, but soon realised it wasn't for him.

'I was in class from 8 to 5, at badminton training three times a week and playing tournaments at weekends. We were expected to do 300 hours of practical work for the course as well. So the following year I moved to Jo'burg to work and study marketing management part-time.'

He shared none of Robin's interests. Robin had long suspected that Gavin was gay, which was simply not okay in his world, or his father's.

'I realised long before Megs that Gavin was gay,' says Robin. 'I mean what kind of a guy has so many girlfriends and nothing going on with them? The way he walked, the way he talked, the way he did things. When he finally came out, I thought: Ja, for sure.'

In 2012, an article in the *Saturday Star* and *Weekend Argus* had Robin wanting to sue. They'd lifted all their information from an episode of *60 Minutes*. But they'd made a typo, substituting Robin for Gavin.

> Robin drops a bombshell – he is gay.
>
> 'It doesn't make you any different. I mean I still live life the way I did before. The only difference now, instead of hooking up with a girl, I get with a guy – so there's no difference really. And yeah, the world's perception sometimes does get in the way, but at the same time I can still get up and beat the crap out of you if you've got something to say.'

Robin was unimpressed. Gavin found his indignation amusing. Breaking the news of his sexual orientation to his conservative family had taken a lot of chutzpah. He'd decided to do it as publicly as possible, on Facebook, on the day of Gay Pride 2009.

Living on Johannesburg's East Rand, he would socialise at a club called Ramp Divas. It was fun – they'd have competitions and win titles. As 'Mr Elegance' for March, Gavin and some of the other title-holders of the year were going to represent the club at the Gay Pride parade in October. On the morning of the procession, he and a friend – another titleholder – typed up an announcement to post on Facebook.

'Before that no one in my family knew I was gay. I thought, "Oh God, what is the reaction going to be?" After the weekend, Megs called me at work and said we need to talk. I eventually phoned her back and she asked me what on earth this was all about. She was a bit hurt that I'd dropped a bombshell. And there were a few ruffled family feathers that I made it so public. Peter, my Granddad, was the most accepting and gracious.'

Megs now says she doesn't have a problem with Gavin being gay. But at the time, estranged from Robin, her immediate thought was that she was unlikely to ever have grandchildren to kiss and cuddle. She felt she'd failed, that she'd been unable to create an environment in which they could all be a big happy extended family.

★

'I am the son of a legend...'

Robin hero-worshipped his father and after he left Megs to live with Dave, they spent quality time together. They would go fishing and hunting bush pig in the Karkloof forest, off-road biking in the Drakensberg.

Dave had known his other children since they were born, but this relationship was different. 'We had to do a lot together in a short time,' he says. 'We broke through a lot. He spoke to me about stuff he'd never told anyone. He made me feel like my opinion mattered, that he put great value to things I told him, that my advice was good advice.'

But newfound relationship with his son or not, Dave was itching to get back to the bush. He applied to manage a game farm at Sondelani Safaris, a 12 000 hectare property about 125 km from Beit Bridge on the main Bulawayo road

'I felt I couldn't live in South Africa. I needed to be in miles and miles of bush. And I didn't think Rob should go with us because there would be nothing for him to do there. I told him to finish the taxidermy course then join us. There was plenty of work for taxidermists in Bulawayo. He wasn't happy, but he agreed and I arranged for him to stay with Katy, his girlfriend, and her parents.'

Dave got the job and Robin went up with him and Nikki to help with the move. After a week, Dave drove him to Messina to catch a bus back to Maritzburg. Rob felt alone.

'All my life I'd been pulled between Sandy and Megs, and all my life I had longed to know my dad,' he says. 'Then I finally got to live with him. I got to know my grandmother, Margaret, and even though she'd had a stroke and couldn't talk, we communicated. Then, after less than a year, Dave was off and I had no family again. The distance between Zimbabwe and Howick seemed very wide.'

It was on that return trip to the border that Dave saw a new side to his son. They were driving slowly along in his old Land Rover, through miles of bush when he noticed Robin looking out of the window, not moving – for a long time.

'It was very quiet in the car, with the bush all around us,' remembered Dave. 'I put my hand on his shoulder and asked him if he was okay. He nodded, then turned to me and cried. Cried like I've never heard a boy cry. I stopped the car and he sobbed and sobbed and sobbed. I hadn't seen him cry before. He was a tough hard kid. This just broke me. We sat by the side of the road for a very long time and he just held me. He couldn't let go. He cried and said he loved me and couldn't handle being on his own again. He felt like he'd been on his own his whole life. It was a part of Rob I'd never seen.'

★

Back in Maritzburg, Megs had no idea that Dave had, in her words, 'abandoned' Robin. Although she'd shut him out of her life, she thought about him all the time.

'Robin leaving played over and over in my mind. When he left I was angry and became emotionally withdrawn. Gradually I begrudgingly came to realise how hard it must have been for him. He'd been eager to please when he got here and I had tried to cram 15 years of discipline, culture and love into a small window as fast as I could so he would be equipped to make his way into the world. In my heart I was trying to make up for all the time I had lost. I wanted him to have the same morals and standards that I'd taught Gavin. Robin had never lived in a properly planned and organised environment.'

Then her sister Pat, who'd kept contact with Robin, told her Dave had gone back to Zimbabwe. Pat arranged a meeting at the Wimpy in Howick.

'I didn't bother telling him to go back to school,' Megs says. 'He would never have. He'd grown up, even changed his name to Lotter. Robin Lotter.'

By now Robin had split up with his girlfriend Katy and found a new home. With natural charm inherited from his father and Sandy's street-wise edge, he had the ability to inveigle his way into people's lives and create new circumstances for himself.

Nikki saw how alike he was to his father: 'Rob's a charmer like his dad, they both talk the talk ... they have the ability to make people feel special, particularly women.'

Megs noticed another similarity: 'Actually, Robin, like Sandy, plays on your emotions and has the ability to make you feel sorry for him.'

He moved in with a friend and his family. He was earning a few thousand rand a month doing taxidermy and could afford to pay a small amount of rent. Megs was hurt that he hadn't told her he'd had nowhere to stay.

'I was quite sore that Rob didn't contact other family members, like my dad who had an empty house after my mum died. He would have welcomed him. It would have made us all happy.'

Robin disagrees: 'It wasn't an option. I couldn't contact them just because I was in trouble. Anyway I thought that Megs had written me off – that she didn't want to be my mother.'

★

In Zimbabwe, Dave found himself in trouble again. The owner of Sondelani Safaris was connected to ZANU-PF and ran a thriving operation that included training elephant captured from the wild. It was a practice frowned on in conservation circles. The elephant would be captured from game parks, with the tacit approval of Zimbabwean politicians, and subjected to cruel training methods, which included chaining them by one leg so they became submissive. Once trained, they'd be used for elephant-backed safaris. Dave found himself caught up with a company that employed methods he didn't approve of. Once he made that known, it was clear he was no longer welcome at Sondelani.

After an incident in which a gun was held to his head, Dave and Nikki decided to get the hell out. They moved back to South Africa and settled in Louis Trichardt. Dave was to help a friend run a hunting establishment at Malapati, just across the border. They planned to organise hunting tours from South Africa into southern Zimbabwe. Robin, who had finished his taxidermy course, joined them and began helping Dave with the hunts and helped set up the camps. They had a concession from a local chief to hunt on tribal land.

Robin liked Louis Trichardt and loved the on-the-go lifestyle, moving between South Africa and Zimbabwe. And being with his father again.

On one occasion, Dave was in South Africa, Rob in Zimbabwe when a chief sent word that he had problem elephant too close to his village destroying maize fields. As they camped and hunted on his land it wasn't a request they could refuse. Robin, who'd never shot an elephant, took Dave's .375 rifle, and set off with two local professional hunters – PHs. They waited at the chief's house until the elephant returned for their afternoon feast.

'There were three of them,' says Robin, 'and we decided to shoot the biggest male. He was standing there, having eaten all the food around him. I was about ten metres away and aimed for his ear and fired. As I reloaded, the second PH shot him again with his 416. The other two elephant ran off and the PH fired a few shots after them so they wouldn't come back. Elephant have good memories. I know it sounds cruel but that's what happens when you live in and around wild animals. The tusks went to National Parks and the villagers ate the meat. I'd never seen so many people just appear from nowhere. No one took any meat until the chief said they could.'

Robin had shot his first elephant and wanted to tell his father. But it was another 10 days before Dave came to fetch him, by which time the diesel for the generator had run out and a peed-off Robin was braai-ing geese to eat.

★

It seems ironic that Robin, a free spirit, who couldn't be tied down by either of his mothers, would enter into the confines of marriage and fatherhood by the age of 22. He met Liezl Hoyer while shopping at the agricultural supplies business where she worked in Louis Trichardt.

Liezl was smitten: 'He walked in with his dad. I could see by the way they were dressed that they were hunters. We made eye contact and he came up to me at the till and started talking in English about the weather. I thought "Oh shit" because my English was bad. He was very charming.'

Robin thought she was beautiful: 'When I saw her I wanted to talk to her, but couldn't think what to say so just started talking about the weather. I told her I was going on a hunt the next day, but would come see her when I was back. Then when we got to the car my Dad said – don't be an idiot, go and get her phone number.'

Liezl laughs: 'A few minutes later he came back and asked for my number. I took a piece of paper and pressed it on his back and wrote my number down. He said he was going to Zimbabwe for two weeks and that we should have a drink when he came back. Minutes later I received a call and then I had his number.'

Two weeks later Dave came into the shop. He had a note from Rob:

'I am hunting elephant and buffalo. The hunt is taking longer than I thought. You are very beautiful. Please don't get a boy-friend. I really like you. Please write back.'

Dave left before she could reply. One night, a month later, Rob phoned saying he was back from Zimbabwe, could he come and fetch her? It was after 10 o'clock and she lived with her mother:

'I loved that he was so spontaneous – but I was a bit scared too. I was an only child with a dark secret hanging over me. But I went with him. Dave was driving – I think they'd had a bit to drink. We drove about 15 km out of town through a forest to where they lived in the mountains. When we got to their house I met Nikki for the first time. She didn't look pleased at all and had words with Dave. Rob took me to his room. I could see he was crazy about hunting. I could smell tanned skins and there were warthog heads on the wall.'

Liezl had had a traumatic childhood with an abusive bipolar father. She'd hidden the sexual abuse from everyone, left home in primary school and gone to live with her maternal grandparents, only reconciling with her mother in high school.

She could relate to Robin and his unusual upbringing. About a month after they started dating, he picked her up and took her to a park in Louis Trichardt and told her about the accident of his birth.

Liezl listened, fascinated. 'I really liked him; he made me feel amazing and I knew I wanted to be with him for the rest of my life, so this news didn't change anything, it made him more interesting.'

In July 2009, Nikki and Dave went to Howick while Liezl and Rob looked after the house in the mountains. It was then that he told her that Dave's partner had lost his concession and could no longer operate his safari company in Zimbabwe. They would be moving back to Howick in September. Rob would go with them.

'I felt heartbroken and angry that he wanted to go with them,' said Liezl, 'but I tried to enjoy the last weeks together.'

In August, Liezl's father, from whom she was estranged, committed suicide. She was distraught, despite the childhood she'd had with him.

'I thought he had a lot of chances to try to make things right. There were many things I still wanted to say to him,' she mourned.

★

Rob got a job welding in Howick, but returned to Limpopo that Christmas. Liezl visited him in the Natal Midlands in February 2010. It was her first plane flight. They stayed at a B&B where Nikki was working.

In the next two weeks she came to realise that Dave and Nikki weren't keen on their relationship. And suspected Rob may have been seeing other girls.

She began wondering what she was getting herself into when she overheard a telephone screaming match he was having with someone. Clearly he had a temper too. Move on, she thought, and went back to Louis Trichardt, determined to forget about him. But by April 2010 Rob had left Howick and was back in Louis Trichardt – and back in her life. The following year she fell pregnant.

'My Mom freaked, then said we must do what we think is right,' says Liezl. 'We told our pastor and he said the right thing was to get married. Rob and I agreed. We both knew that we wanted a family of our own – one that wasn't stuffed up by someone else.'

She began planning their wedding.

'We were scared. But one thing I told him was that he had to make peace with his mother, whether Dave thought she was crazy or not.'

Megs was surprised when she got the call.

'We had tried to patch things up once or twice, but I still had my wall of protection around me and was pretty cool. He'd phone me full of bravado as if he wanted me to see how well he was doing without me and we'd end up arguing. I knew he'd been trying to speak to me for a few weeks, but we'd kept missing each other. I would be in a meeting and then I'd phone back and he was busy. Finally he got hold of me and said: "Mom, I'm getting married next Saturday." He assured me they'd been planning to get married anyway, now it was just happening sooner rather than later.'

Megs attended the wedding. Dave did not. He and Nikki did their best to discourage Robin from getting married. They didn't think that two damaged souls were good ingredients in a recipe for happiness.

'Dave and Nikki flipped,' says Liezl. 'They gave us a lecture and told us we were making a mistake.'

'I didn't want him having my life,' says Dave, 'with lots of kids at a young age, making up for a family life he'd missed out on. He was trying to be something that he wasn't. He wasn't put on earth to help damaged people heal. When I tried to talk to him about it he wouldn't.'

On the Friday night before the wedding the following day, Megs, her father Peter, brother Geoff, sister Pat and niece Lorraine drove to Louis Trichardt, arriving in the early hours. The first glimpse Megs had of her new daughter-in-law was when she walked down the makeshift aisle in the veld.

'She's very attractive and made a beautiful bride,' Megs says. 'It was very touching: they'd written their own vows and a flautist and a guitarist provided the music. We drove straight back to Pietermaritzburg after the ceremony, exhausted from lack of sleep, but with hope in my heart for a possible reconciliation.'

Robin and Liezl's baby arrived five months later, in September 2011. Robin had resolved to write his firstborn's name on his foot with a koki as soon as he was born. But as it turned out, James Jarrod Lotter was the only baby born in the Zoutpansberg Hospital that day, so he didn't have to.

Robin told *YOU* in October 2013: 'About a week after James was born, I thought what would I do now if told I had to give him back? I might have been able to then, but last week he turned two years old – just a little older than I was when the swap was discovered. Then I realised how hard it must be. I wouldn't give him back, no chance. I'd go a step further. I wouldn't want to get to know my own child.'

Megs winced when she read the article. How could he say that? She hated it when the family appeared in local media. She could tolerate *60 Minutes* because the programmes were broadcast in Australia only and not shown online.

It was only through such articles and Facebook that Sandy found out anything about the boy she'd brought up, the boy who'd been her daughter's brother.

Jessica had been close to Robin. 'Initially, I wanted to know about him when he left, but that faded,' she says. 'He kind of faded out of my life. We hardly ever heard from him, so I forgot about him.'

He'd come to visit them once, en route to Louis Trichardt to stay with Dave.

'When he came back I was interested to see how he had changed,' says Jessica. 'He seemed more driven, more organised. I just sat there observing him.'

Then he disappeared out of their lives again.

After they were married, he and Liezl drove down from Louis Trichardt to Pietermaritzburg. Megs suggested they break the journey in Johannesburg and go and visit Sandy. Robin phoned her and said he wanted to introduce them to his wife. Could they spend the night? Sandy asked her mother, whose house it was, and told him it wasn't convenient.

'Kay said there was no way they could spend the night,' she explains. 'He was just using us, like he always had, because he needed somewhere to stay. She was tired of him coming in and out of our lives and upsetting us.'

Megs was surprised by her response. 'I could have arranged for them to stay with friends in Jo'burg,' she says. 'I thought it would be a nice gesture.'

In the end, Robin and Liezl spent the night with a family in Kliprivier he'd known as a child. But he wanted to show Liezl where he'd grown up, so took her round to Daleside the next day. They all seemed to be living in the lounge. After a short while in a gloomy house that seemed to be crumbling around their ears, they left.

'It was so run down, the termites had just about carried it away. It was depressing,' says Robin.

Sandy elaborates: 'It was winter and we had only one heater so we were sleeping on a mattress in the lounge. They didn't stay long.'

'The house smelled like animals and our tea and coffee was full of ants. I felt sorry for all of them. And sorry for Rob that he had grown up there. Jessica just sat there not saying anything,' says Liezl.

Jessica says Robin's visits affected Sandy.

'I miss the person my mother used to be when Robin was here and the way she used to be when Robin was around. She was definitely happier. His leaving changed her. It was like she had lost a son.'

Jessica, once a happy, loving child, is introverted and withdrawn.

'I don't hold attachments any more,' she says. 'I don't have any friends, any close relationships. Johan, my boyfriend, is the only attachment I have. We met on a chat site. When I was in primary school I had a circle of friends, then I went to high school and Robin left and everything just changed. I just thought friendships are not worth anything. I drifted away from everyone.'

Robin was upset when he heard that Jessica had quit school. Once she'd wanted to be an air hostess, later an advocate.

'When I heard Jess had left school too I freaked. I said, "You gotta be shitting me?" She was so clever. I phoned her and told her to come to Limpopo. I told her she could stay with us and look for a job.'

Jessica thought he was really hypocritical. 'He left school before finishing, why shouldn't I?' she protests. 'And I wasn't clever – it's just that he was completely non-academic so everyone seemed clever in comparison. I considered his offer of going to Louis Trichardt, but how could I also leave my mom? I couldn't do what he did to her. If someone asks me if I have brothers or sisters I say no.'

Four Adults Meet

In January 2015, 24 years since they first decided they would try and work as a family – and failed – Megs, Sandy, Robin and Gavin meet up in Johannesburg. Once again *60 Minutes* has brought them together. The venue is a suburban garden. Robin and Megs arrive first. He's flown in from Polokwane, she from Pietermaritzburg. They don't see each other often, but they are slowly rebuilding their relationship.

Louis Trichardt is nine hours from Pietermaritzburg by road, and with three children Robin spends most of his time trying to make ends meet. When he's not taking hunters into the bush, he builds hunting rigs for 4 x 4s. Being here has caused ructions. He has a job he should be finishing and Liezl doesn't see why he should come all this way for an interview. Megs is happy, delighted to have him with her, and wants to know all about her grandchildren.

He tells her how different their characters are – James is easy-going, Daniel has a temper, like him – and about the sheep and pot-bellied pig they have on their plot outside Louis Trichardt.

Megs has her laptop and shows him photographs of the last holiday they spent with her, before Olivia was born, when they took the boys to Salt Rock. Robin remembers the itinerary she drew up for their visit.

'She's a control freak,' he laughs. 'She even emailed it to us before we arrived – what we would do each day. I had to tell her to relax. You can't plan well with kids.'

Megs never lets things ride and is quick to defend herself. Things get expensive if you don't plan and budget for each day, she says. Plus Rob had complained he was bored last time he came to visit.

Robin stops listening. He's restless, not used to sitting around and waiting, unless it's for game on a hunt. He needs some gel for his hair if he's going to be on camera and wanders inside to find some.

The television crew sets up in the garden: four chairs in a semicircle and one facing them for presenter Tara Brown, who will do the interview. She's talking to producer Gareth Harvey, who was on the Mount Nelson trip when the boys were 11. Soundman Micky Breen remarks that when he first met the boys they'd had no front teeth and he'd had hair. Now they have teeth and he has no hair.

'Please try to reduce my double chins,' Megs jokes with cameraman Mark Munro. She's probably put on 40 kg since the Mount Nelson shoot. The weight gain has aggravated her lymphedema.

She sits in the shade under an umbrella, drinking iced water. She needs to keep her feet up to relieve the pressure. The only thing that really helps is tight and uncomfortable bandages. Wearing shoes is difficult. Even the slipslops she has on cut painfully into her toes, which have deep folds and creases. It's limiting. She'd love to visit her sister Kit in England, but a long flight is virtually impossible.

She's experimented with various treatments, once spending weeks in hospital in Johannesburg. It didn't help long-term, but it marked a turning point in her relationship with Robin.

'It was a lonely time,' she remembers. 'I had one or two old college friends to visit, but didn't really know anyone in Jo'burg and the meds made me quite ill. Then one day Robin pitched up at the hospital with baby Daniel. I was ecstatic and it lifted my spirits tremendously. He'd taken his in-laws to the airport and had schemed with my sister Pat to pay me a surprise visit.'

Robin says when he walked into the hospital and saw the delight on Megs' face he saw the love of a mother for her child. For once, her barrier was down.

Megs says she hadn't realised she had put up this barrier. 'It's just self-preservation, really,' she explains. 'But it had been hindering our relationship. And even when I put it up again, he had seen the true feelings in my heart. I no longer had anything to hide from him.'

A taxi pulls up outside. It's Sandy. Robin hasn't seen her in five years, Megs even longer. Sandy looks uneasy, unsure of what to expect. She's found a job – at a fruit and nut factory – and it's been a mission to get the day off work. Her boss looked at her disbelievingly when she told him she needed to do an interview for *60 Minutes* because her son, who was no longer her son, was swapped at birth a quarter of a century ago.

Gavin is late. He has a job in digital marketing and lives and works north of Johannesburg. It's taken him more than an hour to get here because of a traffic jam caused by the annual Daredevil 5km Run in which thousands of men trot along in Speedos for cancer awareness. He eyes the television crew warily. They remember him; he doesn't appear to remember them. The impression is that he's only doing the interview because Megs wants him to. He treats her as the matriarch; is respectful, and defers to her. At the same time, there's a naturalness to their relationship that Megs wishes she had with Robin. The rift caused by his walking out still weighs on her and has changed her personality, she says. While she doesn't think twice about phoning or messaging Gavin every day, she's cautious with Robin. Sometimes she wishes she'd had another child, her very own whom she could've raised without drama. John even had his vasectomy reversed when she was in her thirties because she'd wanted to fall pregnant, but it hadn't happened.

Gavin hugs Megs and Sandy and gives Robin a cursory greeting. They have what Robin describes as 'a funny relationship', united by circumstances, but nothing else in common. Although they share a birthday, they don't contact one another on the day. It's not a time of celebration, more a reminder of the painful and perplexing mistake of their birth.

Later, Gavin ventures an explanation: 'He is in theory my brother, we share the same families. But if someone asks me if I have siblings I usually say it's confusing – would you like the long story, or the short story?'

Robin still thinks Megs made the wrong choice all those years ago, keeping Gavin and leaving him with Sandy.

'Gavin's saving grace is that he grew up with Megs and Granny and Granddad,' he says. 'If he'd stayed with Sandy, he would never have risen above his circumstances.'

Gavin shrugs: 'Maybe he's right, maybe I wouldn't have been able to get myself out of there. But what would Robin have done with my life? It's impossible to say.'

Robin is ambivalent about Sandy: 'I have a lot of insecurities about the way Sandy raised me. She made me make hectic decisions. And even though I am not genetically part of her, we have similarities. I don't like confrontation, thanks to Sandy. Even now when I see her, I still feel I need to forgive her. When I have an issue with one of my boys, I have to stop myself from losing it like Sandy used to lose it with me.'

Gavin prefers not to think about what his life would have been like as Sandy's son. What's the point? 'Get over it, accept, move on and make peace with it,' he tells Robin once the *60 Minutes* cameras are rolling. He sits on the end, next to Sandy, mother and son, and the similarities are obvious. Both have the same hazel eyes, but sound very different when they open their mouths. Gavin's accent is posh Natal, Sandy's flat East Rand. Curiously, she's removed a ring he was wearing on his middle finger and placed it on her thumb. He looks like he wants it back, but is too polite to say anything. Tara Brown addresses Robin:

Tara Brown: 'Robin, you said the last time we met with you that if you discovered that your own son was not your son you would not try to seek out the other child, that you would accept what you had. Have you changed your mind?'

Robin: 'Yes I did say that. But time has changed me. I have gotten to know my own son and there is no

159

way in the world I would not want to know my own child, my own flesh and blood.'

Tara: 'Megs, what is upsetting you?'

Megs: 'Just thinking about it. It hasn't all been bad.'

Tara: 'So why are you crying?'

Megs: 'Because it's just so sad. Your feelings change all the time. As Robin just said, the first time he said he wouldn't want to know his child. Now he feels differently. We never knew if we were going to lose the kids or keep them, we felt so insecure. How do you tell your real child you didn't want to know them? And how do you walk away from the child you've known for two years? Sandy and I were victims and wanted to do what was best. There are times we haven't spoken, but we will always have a connection, no matter what. We might've been fighting, but we had a bond and still do.'

Sandy: 'Fortunately we have always thought along the same lines, although not always agreed.'

Tara: 'What do you feel about this latest baby swap at another Johannesburg Hospital? At the moment the parents don't agree, one wants to swap, the other doesn't. The courts have decided they must stay where they are.'

Megs: 'Gavin and Robin were just short of two and Sandy and I had bonded with them in a way that we couldn't separate ourselves from them. So how can you at the age of four? I can't understand a parent saying they prefer one child above the other. Children have a right to their natural parents, but they have to feel secure.'

Tara: 'Right now those mothers feel they will never have peace again. Do you think they will?'

Sandy: 'Those mothers are going to have to form some kind of relationship with one another where they can sit and work things out together and put the children's best interests first. Then you can't go wrong.'

Megs: 'They are fortunate they live in the same area. Sandy and I lived in two different provinces with different influences. The basics are there for these mothers to make a plan, to find peace.'

Tara: 'Are you all at peace now?'

Robin: 'That's a hard question for me to answer. I left Sandy when I was 15 and there are certain things in my life I will never get over. Maybe they made me a stronger person, maybe not. But sometimes they crop up and I battle. It all gets too much for me. Part of me will always think that another human being is living the life I would've had and vice versa. For me there is always that question: what would it have been like?'

Tara: 'And you will never find an answer. Gavin?'

Gavin: 'Look, I can understand where he is coming from. If I'd gone home with Sandy from that hospital, who would I be today? But what's the point of questioning it? Robin might have had dreams, but he has a family now and three damn adorable children. Accept, move on, as I said, I made peace with it all years ago.'

Robin hasn't made peace with it. When he was 19 he considered suing the state for trauma suffered in his upbringing as a result of the swap. But legal advice was that it would be almost impossible to prove the source of the trauma. Who's to say it wasn't caused by the decision not to switch back? He was disappointed not to get his day in court.

*

Months after the interview reunion, back in Pietermaritzburg, Megs prepares herself for Robin's eventual return. She wants to get it right this time. Ten years have passed since he drove away from here with his father. Now she wants him to come home with his family. Times are tough in Louis Trichardt. He's borrowed money and unless he works all day and most of the night, he doesn't bring in enough. And if he works all the time, or goes off for weeks with overseas hunters, Liezl takes strain coping with three children under the age of five.

So Megs and John are painting the bedrooms.

'This room for the boys, James and Daniel … Olivia will sleep in my arts and crafts room. We are going to make her a doll's house – I've already bought a little tea set for it. Robin and Liezl will have Gavin's old room, he won't mind… There's hope in me that one day they will come here and I will get to know my grandchildren. I won't hold my breath, but we could give them a lot of support here… If it doesn't happen, John and I must think seriously about where we are going to retire…'

In Daleside, Sandy ponders how to save her mother's house from the auctioneer's hammer. Her old car stands in the yard, out of petrol. She's lost her job at the fruit and nut factory. If only she could get some capital, she could become an online currency trader, she thinks. She might make enough to afford a new place. She has another job interview this week … maybe …

And so they dream …

★

Six months later, a laden truck and trailer pulls into Megs' driveway in Pietermaritzburg. Two little boys spill out, followed by their mother, father and baby sister. It's been a 12-hour drive and Robin and Liezl look exhausted. James was carsick and they had to keep stopping. Little Olivia is less than a year old.

Megs can't believe it's finally happened. She didn't allow herself to believe it until she knew they'd left Louis Trichardt.

'The suspense was killing me,' she breathed. 'I had permanent stomach pains.'

Robin had phoned at three that morning to say they were having trouble fitting everything in and were going to postpone until they'd hired a bigger trailer. She'd freaked out, thinking they had no intention of coming. She took a sleeping pill. When she woke up the sun was high in the sky and there was a message on her phone saying they'd arrived in Johannesburg and had stopped for breakfast. The week before, her nephew Christopher, Geoff's 23-year-old son, had been killed on his way to work on his motor-bike. The family was devastated and Megs was feeling fragile. She worried about the long car journey, but was acutely aware that she was being given a second chance to live under the same roof as her biological son. With a few strings attached…

'This time I am not going into this with rose-tinted spectacles. I expect us to have differences. We must just allow each other time-out. At least he and Liezl won't be short of baby-sitters here. I need to start reading to those kids, the earlier the better. I have pulled out *Jemima Puddle Duck* for tonight. There is lots of family support here, but Rob will miss the hunting. For now, his family must come first. I am hoping they can get back on their feet and put aside some savings while living with me. We will need to give a bit to make it work for a while. If they aren't happy, they can move on.'

She's put the little boys in Robin's old room. Robin and Liezl are in Gavin's room, which Gavin has mixed feelings about. In one breath he says 'awesome' because he knows how happy it will make Megs; in the next, he says he wants his old room back at Christmas.

164

Being a father hasn't eased Rob's restlessness. Forty-eight hours after arriving, he's cleaned out the garage, a task neglected by John who seems to spend most of his time with his Maltese poodle on his lap, watching sport on television. Megs keeps a wary eye on her son.

'We have to watch him,' she confides. 'He throws out our stuff without asking. I have to keep him away from my craft room.'

But Robin gets stuck into stuff that John has neglected forever and a day. He's planning to go back to Louis Trichardt in a month for a hunting job, but after Cecil the lion is shot in Zimbabwe, Robin's overseas hunters cancel because of the negative publicity. He's disappointed. He misses the bushveld. He goes back anyway to fetch his Land Rover. Then takes it to Badplaas in Mpuma-langa, where Dave and Nikki now live, to store it there until he needs it.

Dave isn't impressed that Robin hasn't been able to make a go of it in Louis Trichardt and has gone home to Mum: 'I warned him about making the same stupid mistakes I did. Having kids young, borrowing money to make ends meet. You need maturity to deal with children and marriage,' he says.

He's warned Robin not to repeat the sins of their childhoods: 'My dad used to thrash me as a child and Robin used to get beaten. I've told him to break the cycle; he must never use a belt on his kids. He must get rid of his anger and hate and deal with life with love in his heart. Go for counselling if that's what it takes.'

Rob and Liezl have been for counselling and worked through a lot, she says: 'About a year into our marriage I started realising that other things were more important to him: money, pleasing people. He was afraid of disappointing people. I think that's because he was robbed of his childhood. Sandy didn't teach him how to save, how to work with money, how to be responsible. He learnt survival tricks instead and how to lie. He gets into debt easily and is obsessed with money.'

When Robin phoned to tell Sandy he was moving to Pietermaritzburg again she was surprised and a little bitter: 'Megs has got her own way again… I wonder what she promised him this time. And why they think it will work this time round?'

Jessica listens to her wearily, tired of the effect Robin continues to have on her mother, more than a decade since he left them: 'I really hope that not too far in the future my mother will be able to get over this entire incident, be able to move on with her life, be able to carry on instead of being stuck in the past. I know when things from the past come up and how she reacts to them. Robin moving back down to Pietermaritzburg … I don't know how that is going to affect her now, but I know she will be affected,' she says.

Last Words

From Sandy to the boys

Becoming a mother was to me one of the most precious events any woman could experience. It meant a total change in my life. I would be responsible for another person's well being. It would mean sacrificing lazy Saturday afternoons to look after someone, but it didn't really upset me. I chose to be a mother because I wanted to; I wanted to share this wonderful world, full of nature and adventures. Okay, I admit circumstances weren't perfect – there was no big bank account or the very best baby gear, but I knew I could do it. I wanted to do it.

Once I had my baby in my arms at home I was happy. I had a job, I felt stable and secure. Yes, he was colicky, but I nursed him through that, even though my breast milk did not agree with him at all.

It was a joy and a pleasure being a mom. Then at 22 months the world seemed to stop revolving.

Time and time again I have gone back to that hospital in my head: how could they have put both newborn babies in one incubator without tagging them? Why was my boy not tagged before his umbilical cord was cut?

My biggest regret is that I didn't insist. His hair was darker, he looked much bigger than the baby they gave me. I should've trusted my instincts when I walked into that nursery. I would've had a son today.

Instead I found myself labelled a bad mother because I could not provide materially. I found myself blamed for bad report cards. And I found myself depressed. Something I had never suffered before. And now I have a daughter who is withdrawn and depressed too. It ruined her innocent life.

Over the years I have found myself thinking about you two time and time again, realising that you were growing up and wondering how you were growing up. But it felt like you had been taken from me. I was once close to you, but I became far from you.

Boys – you are both mature and I do believe intelligent young men. Always remember a coin has two sides. Flip the coin and study the other side intently and make up your own minds.

I hope that you don't have to make choices and that you never go through what we went through. I hope that you have happy lives and that they turn out the way you want them to. Remember it just takes a careless instant to change life forever.

Love
Mom

From Megs

'My children were switched at birth.' It sounds like the title of a fictitious TV drama. But it happened to me. A lot has been said about it and there have been many repercussions and recriminations as well as countless delights and experiences that have brought us to our current status.

I had hoped that the process of relating our story for this book might have been a chance at reconciliation. But I fear that it has instead created a new set of resentments with the chance of reconciliation becoming a distant probability.

The media has played a large role of support and conflict particularly where the economic circumstances have been highlighted and misrepresented creating a platform of mistrust and envy and a huge chasm between the boys which should never have been there.

Although Sandy and my relationship has for the most part been fraught with unease, distrust and trauma we have a bond, a kinship. We once had a common purpose and a love of the same children. Even now, after everything, I feel the need to communicate with her if I hear of a similar switch – we were both victims of a rare occurrence and few know what it feels like.

In September 2015 I read about two baby boys who were switched at birth at a hospital in El Salvador. I immediately thought of Sandy. This swap was discovered early and the children were swapped back before a judge when they were just a few months old. Could they have done it if their boys were toddlers, like ours?

Every incident like this makes me acutely aware of how often and easily this can happen. Who knows how many of the hundreds of babies born every day at hospitals in South Africa are switched?

It's mind-blowing that measures haven't been put in place since our incident. The whole point of us going to court was to make hospitals more vigilant. My advice to mothers is to go with your gut feeling – if you suspect there is something wrong, act on it. Nurses must listen and trust those mothers who say something is wrong. It would save a lot of heartache for those who do, by chance, find out months or years down the line. You have the right to bring up your own child.

I guess like anyone who has experienced heartache you learn to continue with your life and get on with the business of living and hope that you have made a difference.

I am grateful that Rob got to know his dad. I had always wanted that despite what others have said. I have forgiven Dave and hope for my part that he has forgiven me.

I wish the boys had a better relationship with each other and with Jessica as she has been the biggest loser in all of this. I am sorry that Sandy blames me for her predicament, but the switch happened to me too. I was also a very traumatised victim who was not well off and with few resources, except a very supportive extended family and the will to try and do the very best for my children. My determination helped me to establish relationships with both my children even though at times it seemed impossible and the hurt was unbearable.

What happened to me taught me to swallow my pride and open my heart – through this I was able to salvage my relationship with my son Robin, gain a daughter-in-law and three gorgeous grandchildren. My relationship with Gavin is as strong as ever and I have gained a lifelong champion. What wonderful men they have become. My life is fuller and richer for all of it.

From Robin

Over the last few years I've made some major life decisions and changes – some good and some bad. On reflection, I can definitely say that I have learned a lot from all the people who have had an input in my life, good and bad. Even though I am grateful for where I am today, being a husband and a father to three beautiful children, I often feel judged because of the decisions that I have made in my life – I probably feel that way because I have had so many insecurities about my identity. At least today I can say I know who I want to be and am trying to reach that goal.

Through this whole swapped-at-birth thing, I really felt like I was the black sheep or was treated like one. I had to make big life decisions from a very young age. Decisions like leaving Sandy to live with my biological mother to get to know her better (the one thing my heart so desired), then I left Megs to go stay with my dad because of complications and my need to break free because I didn't want to feel tied down by Megs' rules. From there, I had to move again to stay with a girlfriend, then a friend.

It felt like a lot of huge decisions were dumped on my shoulders and they became a big burden in my life. I became depressed and a nervous wreck, forgetful and just plain wise-ass because I already felt like I had to be the grown-up when I was still a young boy and man. There were always things changing in my life in a big way – like what's Rob going to do next?

It felt for most of my life like I was on my own. I feel it was a bit unfair for me as a young boy – not even a man yet – to have to make very hard life decisions, when an adult should've made them. But then again, what is ever the right decision? And I know one should not have regrets. The way my life is today, I can say that all the drama, hardships and frustration, along with major life decisions, have all worked out for me. But I do ask myself why it had to get that extreme for me to get where I am today.

From Gavin

'Oh my word, that sounds like a movie' or 'I can't believe it, are you okay? When did you find out?' are the usual responses that I get when I tell people that I was switched at birth. What people don't seem to realise, is that I am who I am today because of my past. Things would have been different if I had grown up with Sandy and Jessica and my grandmother Kay, and the person I would have become would more than likely be the polar opposite of who I am.

It is because of the love, support and acceptance of my 'family' that I have been given the opportunity to exceed not only their expectations, but also my own. To be my own person regardless of sexuality, family ties or the mistakes that I have made. They are the reason that I am who I am, that I have the strength to accept my life and why I am able to see this situation as black and white, with no grey areas.

Robin and I grew up with full knowledge of the swap, and to this day we can understand why our mothers did what they did and kept the children that they had. I will however not apologise for being given the life that I have, as all that I have received – what people think has been just given to me – I have actually worked for. I was taught discipline and self-restraint by my loving grandmother Joan; I was taught acceptance by the family as a whole from Geoff, Kit, Pat, Laurie and Peter, as well as all my cousins. I worked to achieve the grades I did in school, I worked even harder to achieve my accolades in sports, but people think that this is just something that I was given due to being raised in a 'wealthy' family.

The relationships that I have now with my family are proof that blood is not always thicker than water. There has however been a strain in my personal relationships, because of the afore-mentioned speculation. And due to the 'debacle' that is our lives, trust is not something that I give easily.

Irrespective of the above, I have my family to thank for allowing me to grow into the person that I am today. For the world, the perception is that I was raised in 'affluence' thanks to an Austra-lian TV crew who decided to set my grandparents' achievements as the backdrop to my life. However, there were times that dinner was samp and beans. Megs worked day in and day out to make sure that there was always food on the table, but according to international reports we were living the high life. It is because of this false reporting that resentment brewed in the relationship between Robin and me.

I wish to leave a thought with each of you: Most people feel that they are able to judge based on their own experiences. How-ever, looking back now, the precedent has been set – by us. If you were to discover that your child had been switched after 18 months, if you had spent 18 months loving, nurturing and car-ing for a child, would you be so willing to give up that child in the hopes that it would make everything better or go away? Or would you fight to know your biological child, as well as the child you had raised for 18 months?

Lightning Source UK Ltd.
Milton Keynes UK
UKHW022217201121
394320UK00005B/566